LOYALTY IN
A DEMOCRATIC STATE

Problems in American Civilization

READINGS SELECTED BY THE
DEPARTMENT OF AMERICAN STUDIES
AMHERST COLLEGE

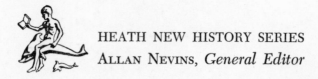

HEATH NEW HISTORY SERIES
ALLAN NEVINS, *General Editor*

LOYALTY IN
A DEMOCRATIC STATE

EDITED WITH AN INTRODUCTION BY

John C. Wahlke

Problems in American Civilization

READINGS SELECTED BY THE
DEPARTMENT OF AMERICAN STUDIES
AMHERST COLLEGE

D. C. HEATH AND COMPANY: Boston

INTRODUCTION

NEVER has the problem of political loyalty troubled Americans as deeply as it does today. Such names as Alger Hiss, Senator McCarthy, Owen Lattimore, William Remington, Whittaker Chambers, or Senators Mundt and Nixon have become as familiar as the names of the nation's presidents. In the press, in national, state, and local legislatures and executive offices, and in public and private discussions, Americans debate such questions as: Should we support the activities of the House Committee on Un-American Activities? Is the McCarran Act a betrayal of American principles of government or an intelligent effort to safeguard them? Are there Communists in key places in the government, in Hollywood, in labor, in industry, or in our schools and colleges, and, if there are, what action (if any) does their presence require of the community? Is the federal government's employee loyalty program serving to protect the integrity of our public servants and our system of government, or is it tending to the destruction of both?

The loyalty problem, thus posed, centers upon the question: What is the legitimate position in the American community of Communists and so-called fellow travelers? But the loyalty problem, in America as elsewhere, is much older than the Communist Party. Tories in the Revolutionary period were required to take loyalty oaths and to submit to other tests of their loyalty; southern Americans in the Civil War and Reconstruction periods were likewise required to prove their right to full membership in the American political community by test oaths and loyalty checks. In these cases, the problem raised was that of clashing political loyalties; the allegedly "disloyal" were suspected of owing allegiance to some political entity other than the American nation.

Historically, however, the problem of loyalty has often involved not a simple clash of political loyalties, but a conflict between different types of loyalty. Such conflicts produced in sixteenth- and seventeenth-century England the long series of test oaths and loyalty checks imposed by Catholic governments upon Protestant Englishmen and by Protestant governments upon Catholic Englishmen. The separation of church and state has not completely eliminated similar conflicts in the United States. The nomination of Catholic Alfred E. Smith for President in 1928 led certain citizens publicly to question whether his religious loyalty might not at times run counter to the political loyalty Americans expect of their chief executive. Governor Smith and many Americans, both Catholic and Protestant, denied such a possibility. The many cases involving conscientious refusal by members of religious sects (Jehovah's Witnesses, for example) to obey certain requirements of the state pose the problem sharply: To what extent may the state require that political loyalty transcend religious loyalty of individual citizens?

Commentators on the current loyalty controversy disagree concerning the relevance of such previous American experiences. Almost every student recognizes that our contemporary problem is intimately associated with the "cold war" between the United States and the Soviet Union. Many feel that the safety of the nation in this struggle requires new and unprecedented measures because, in the words of Morris Ernst, "We are facing an utterly new problem in American life." The new problem, it is felt, is largely the result of the ideological character of the cold war. Again in the words of Morris Ernst, "It is a war for the minds of men, and we can lose it without losing a life." On the other hand, others believe that some or all of the "loyalty measures" taken to safeguard the nation in the cold war reveal ignorance of the lessons of history and violate fundamental democratic principles. This volume is devoted to a consideration of some of the important measures around which this controversy centers: the conviction of eleven Communist leaders under the Smith Act; the federal government's employee loyalty program; the Internal Security Act of 1950 (popularly known as the McCarran Act); and the exclusion of Communists from college teaching.

A fundamental issue underlying discussion of these measures is: What is the meaning of "loyalty," or "disloyalty," in a democracy? All parties to the controversy, it should be emphasized, agree that sabotage, espionage, and acts of treason (as hitherto narrowly defined in criminal statutes and the Constitution) are clearly disloyal. All agree that repeal or "softening" of long-standing laws or constitutional prohibitions against such actions is not an issue in the current loyalty problem.

Beyond this, agreement does not extend. Those who oppose loyalty programs generally maintain that an individual's actions, and not his ideas, constitute the only legitimate test of his loyalty in a democracy. They contend that a democracy can never officially label any ideas "loyal" without ceasing to be a democracy. Persons holding this view frequently offer, as the proper standard by which to judge loyalty, the "clear and present danger doctrine" enunciated by Justice Oliver Wendell Holmes. This doctrine assumes that a democracy must allow all citizens the widest possible latitude for discussing the nature and business of the political community. According to it, the government is justified in interfering in the realm of ideas *only* if the nature of a specific utterance of the ideas and the circumstances in which they are uttered are such as to give rise to a clear and present danger of overt actions which the state may legitimately forbid. By such a standard, it is urged, every American must be considered loyal so long as he engages in no actions which the law specifically forbids. The state may concern itself with the loyalty of its citizens only to the extent of prohibiting such clearly disloyal actions as sabotage, espionage, and treason. Such a standard, it is asserted, does not justify the present loyalty measures. Many feel that these measures are not only unjustifiable but are themselves disloyal because they violate democratic principles, which are said to be the only legitimate objects of political loyalty.

Defenders of the loyalty programs, however, claim that the viewpoint just described is unforgivably naïve in seeking to settle loyalty problems of the present by rigid application of arguments and standards from the past. They assert that complete toleration of undemocratic ideas and organizations is a luxury which the nation can no longer afford, that a democracy today must be willing to regulate and curtail freedom of association and expression, if it is clearly demonstrated that organizations and ideas aim (as Communist organizations and ideas are held to do) at the ultimate destruction of American democracy. They warn that modern techniques of organization and action, which tremendously increase the effectiveness of fifth-column methods, present a clear and present danger to the national security — not merely a danger that loyal citizens will be beguiled by undemocratic notions, but a danger of acts of violence. They warn further that this danger is heightened if persons and organizations that are really agents of a foreign power are permitted to take refuge under the very democratic principles they intend to destroy. Therefore, they say, membership in such organizations as the Communist Party and the holding of beliefs upon which such organizations are based constitute disloyalty which is a grave threat to the continued existence of American democracy. Such a conception of the meaning of loyalty, it is argued, fully justifies such measures as the Smith Act, the McCarran Act, the federal loyalty program, and the exclusion of Communist teachers from American colleges.

This, then, is the fundamental issue: What is the nature of loyalty in a democratic state? Should it be defined only in terms of overt acts of sabotage, espionage, or treason? Or should it be defined in terms which include the non-criminal day-to-day activities, the political faith, and the general philosophy of its citizens? The reader's solution to this fundamental issue will materially influence his answers to other basic issues, which involve applications of his conception of loyalty in assessing the behavior of those accused of subversive activities. Are the actions of such persons clearly disloyal? Or are they merely the exercise of the democratic right to express unpopular ideas? What is the nature and extent of the dangers created by the allegedly disloyal activities? What actions may a democratic government legitimately take to meet these dangers?

The opening selections of this volume are concerned with the basic issues. The first is from *Witch Hunt* by Carey McWilliams, attorney and author of a number of books on such controversial topics as minority rights, racial discrimination, and labor, agricultural, and land policies. It offers a highly condensed exposition of McWilliams's conception of loyalty and his application of that concept in judging current measures. The selection which follows by Arthur M. Schlesinger, Jr., Harvard history professor, author of a Pulitzer Prize–winning history of the Jacksonian period, who is widely known for his support of liberal organizations and causes, presents the view that McWilliams's conceptions, even if valid, are wrongly applied to current affairs. The third selection is the classic statement of the "clear and present danger" doctrine from Justice Holmes's dissenting opinion in *Abrams v. U. S.* Then follow excerpts from two opposing Supreme Court decisions in cases involving instances where religious beliefs of certain citizens led to their being called "disloyal" by others. Both Justice Felix Frankfurter's opinion in the *Gobitis* case,[1] which upholds the right of the state to require pupils to salute the flag even though that ceremony violates their religious beliefs, and Justice Robert H. Jackson's opinion in the *Barnette* case,[2] which denies that right,

[1] *Minersville School District v. Gobitis,* 310 U. S. 586.

[2] *West Virginia State Board of Education v. Barnette,* 319 U. S. 624.

give serious attention to the meaning of loyalty.

A major portion of the book is given over to consideration of the four restrictive measures previously mentioned. The conviction of eleven Communist leaders under the Smith Act is the subject of selections which include the opinion of Mr. Justice Jackson concurring in the Supreme Court decision which upheld the conviction, and the opinion of Justice William O. Douglas dissenting from that decision. The federal employee loyalty program, the second measure considered, is described in the article by Roger S. Abbott, a political scientist who has made an exhaustive study of the program. The program is attacked in the selection by Leonard A. Nikolorić, member of a Washington law firm which has defended many government employees before loyalty boards and in the courts. The program is defended in principle, and suggestions are made for improving it, in the selection by Morris Ernst, a lawyer and author whose concern for civil liberties has long been demonstrated both in his writings and in his legal services for the American Civil Liberties Union. Facts concerning the background and major provisions of the McCarran Act, the third measure presented, are given in the selection by Arthur E. Sutherland, Jr., a member of the faculty of the Harvard Law School. The legislation is defended in excerpts from a speech in the United States Senate by Karl E. Mundt, Republican Senator from South Dakota, who was one of the chief sponsors of the legislation. The case against it is made in President Harry S. Truman's message vetoing the Act. For consideration of the fourth measure, the exclusion of disloyal persons from college teaching, the reader is given the opposing views of two men of long experience in academic work.

Sidney Hook, professor of philosophy at New York University, whose published works include books on education, Marxism, and philosophy, argues that American colleges should not permit Communists on their faculties. Alexander Meiklejohn, former president of Amherst College, teacher, author, and philosopher, holds that the exclusion of Communists from college teaching is unjustified.

In the two concluding selections in this volume, attention is again directed to the general issues. Here historian Henry Steele Commager denounces most of the loyalty measures now in effect as based upon an erroneous conception of the nature of loyalty. J. Edgar Hoover, Director of the F.B.I., contends, on the other hand, that conceptions such as Commager's are, if not erroneous, at least totally inapplicable to the current problem.

Few problems are as vitally important to Americans today as that of loyalty in the democratic state. A right solution to that problem will bulwark democratic government; a wrong one may well seriously weaken it. The solution adopted may affect the outcome of the struggle now being waged between groups of rival powers holding rival ideologies; it will certainly affect directly the lives of many Americans. This volume is designed to help the reader appreciate the complexity of the issues and discover a basis for solution. Its fundamental assumption is that a workable solution is to be found, in a democracy, neither by indifference nor by hysteria on the part of its citizens, but only by their careful and thoughtful study of the problem.

[NOTE: The statement on page xii by Alan Barth is quoted, with permission, from *The Loyalty of Free Men* (New York: The Viking Press, 1951), p. 19.]

CONTENTS

The Clash of Issues

Americans do not agree concerning the necessity for loyalty programs:

A liberal lawyer, Morris Ernst, urges:

"Let's wake up. We are facing an utterly new problem in American life. . . . The old-fashioned spy, who used to bribe the stenographer or fall in love with the boss, is easy to cope with. But we are at war. . . . It is a war for the minds of men, and we can lose it without losing a life."

But author Carey McWilliams says:

"Superficially the American obsession with loyalty appears to stem from the facts and implications of 'the cold war'; but in this respect we could be the victims of a serious delusion. . . . a concern with loyalty has often served as cover for an attack on civil liberties."

There is corresponding disagreement concerning the nature and effect of loyalty programs:

Carey McWilliams argues:

"That we are punishing heresy in the guise of testing loyalty becomes clear the moment we attempt to define the meaning of loyalty."

And historian Henry Steele Commager says:

"What is the new loyalty? It is, above all, conformity. It is the uncritical and unquestioning acceptance of America as it is — the political institutions, the social relationships, the economic practices."

But historian Arthur M. Schlesinger, Jr., disagrees:

"Those who believe that the agitation over communism is only a pretext for purging liberals . . . are themselves mistaking a part for the whole. . . . We face here not just a figment of the reactionary imagination but a proved problem for the security of free nations."

Believers of all shades of view are agreed that some principle must be found for solving the dilemma described by Abraham Lincoln:

"Must a government of necessity be too strong for the liberties of its people, or too weak to maintain its own existence?"

Director of the F.B.I., J. Edgar Hoover, speaks for many who feel that current loyalty measures generally solve the dilemma without doing violence to American principles:

> "I confess to a real apprehension so long as Communists are able to secure ministers of the gospel to promote their evil work and espouse a cause that is alien to the religion of Christ and Judaism. I do fear so long as school boards and parents tolerate conditions whereby Communists and fellow travelers, under the guise of academic freedom, can teach our youth a way of life that eventually will destroy the sanctity of the home, that undermines faith in God, that causes them to scorn respect for constituted authority and sabotage our revered Constitution."

But a Washington correspondent, Alan Barth, cautions:

> "The disloyalty of the Americanists impairs national security more seriously than the comparable disloyalty of the Communists. . . . It is more deeply subversive, strikes more injuriously at the real roots of loyalty and of American strength. It would, in fact, meet the threat of communism by the substitution of Communist techniques for the techniques of freedom."

Carey McWilliams:

THE MODERN AMERICAN WITCH HUNT

THE issuance by President Truman of Executive Order No. 9835 on March 22, 1947, setting up a federal loyalty program, marks the beginning of an American obsession with loyalty that, in broad outline, parallels a similar Russian obsession dating from the "all-out campaign" against the Leningrad Literary Group in August 1946.[1] Since then states, counties, and cities have imitated the federal program; many industries and plants now require affidavits of loyalty from their employees; scores of trade unions have adopted a similar requirement, along with schools and colleges; and, in California, an association of amateur archers now demands an affidavit of loyalty from its members! Not since the time of the Alien and Sedition Acts has the federal government been so intensely and morbidly preoccupied with the loyalty of the American people.

As citizens, we are asked to believe that this preoccupation with *our* loyalty finds immediate justification in a series of "revelations" about spy rings and espionage activities and, generally, in a tense international situation. However, when our officials comment upon the parallel preoccupation of the Soviet government, the mote suddenly obscures the beam. For example, Lieutenant General Walter Bedell Smith, by way of answering the question: "Why were the Soviet

[1] *My Three Years in Moscow* by Lieutenant General Walter Bedell Smith.

authorities so apprehensive about the loyalty of the masses, particularly after the conclusion of a successful war?" points unerringly to the impact of the war upon internal tensions in the Soviet Union. Superficially the American obsession with loyalty appears to stem from the facts and implications of "the cold war"; but in this respect we could be the victims of a serious delusion.

One way to clarify the meaning of the loyalty program is to identify some of the instruments being used to determine who is loyal and who is disloyal. Properly identified, these instruments provide the key to an understanding of the curious psychological warfare which the government has been waging against the people for the last three years. Surely the use of the political court-martial to coerce conformity and the revival in the United States, in the middle of the twentieth century, of the discredited and abhorrent "test oath" should remind us that a concern with loyalty has often served as cover for an attack on civil liberties.

The Matter of Oaths

Allegiance has a different background in America than in England, or, for that matter, in most European countries. With us, the obligation of allegiance is not derived from an oath but from a relationship. "Allegiance and protection," wrote Chief Justice Waite, "are reciprocal obligations. The one is compensation for the

From *Witch Hunt: The Revival of Heresy* by Carey McWilliams, pages 27–32, 33–43, 45, 47–48, 246–250. Copyright 1950 by Carey McWilliams. Reprinted by permission of Little, Brown and Company.

other; allegiance for protection and protection for allegiance." With the British
allegiance remained an aspect of fealty
until they were finally forced to acknowledge, after a long experience with test
oaths, that allegiance to the modern state
rests upon considerations slightly more
complex than the sworn loyalty of a servant to his master. A subject "swears"
allegiance to his sovereign; the allegiance
of American citizens goes to the compact
embodied in the Constitution and derives
from the citizenship conferred by the
Fourteenth Amendment. It does not imply an uncritical acceptance of the foreign policy of the government even in a
critical period nor does it imply ideological conformity. We pledge allegiance to
the flag; not to the profit system. The
growth in democratic understanding implied in the distinction between the allegiance of citizens and the feudal fealty
of subjects is clearly reflected in the
history of the disastrous "test oath"
from which the modern loyalty affidavit
derives.

After the passage of the act vesting the
succession in the heirs of Anne Boleyn,
the words "papist" and "popery" became
devil words with the British Protestants.
The "papists," of course, were "agents of
a foreign power," whose activities were
supposed to be directed by a highly
disciplined "conspiratorial" organization
which, of course, was plotting to overthrow the government "by force and violence." The papists, it was said, evaded
perjury by subtle equivocations and reservations which were encouraged and
condoned by the Jesuits. In the popular
view, the Jesuits were known for their
"secret notions and traitorous practices."[2]
To cope with this situation, a thorough-
going "loyalty program" was inaugu-

rated. Papists could not hold office; they
were banished from the court; they could
only live in certain restricted areas; they
were subject to periodic fines; their prop-
erties could be confiscated; their religious
ceremonies were often prohibited for
long periods; the Catholic party or faction was banned; and individual Catholics faced the constant threat of arrest,
imprisonment, and exile. Officials with
Catholic wives were placed under close
surveillance; proposals to take Catholic
children from their parents were seriously considered; and "mulcts in purse
and person" were levied right and left.
It should be added, also, that Catholic
and Protestant were then partisan political designations. Couched in the idiom
of theology, the struggle was undeniably
political.[3]

When from time to time a high-ranking
British official was identified as having
been a "secret" Catholic, a spasm of fear
swept through high court circles and still
another investigation would be promptly
ordered. But each investigation only gave
rise to new waves of persecution. Incidents such as the celebrated Gunpowder
Plot served to keep the fear of "papist
treachery" alive and the manipulation of
this fear became a major political tactic.
Every crisis in the relations between
Britain and France, or Spain, including,
of course, the persecution of Protestants
by French Catholics, was likely to make
matters more difficult for the Catholics in
England and was invariably cited as justification for further repressions. But historians have noticed that the persecution
of Catholics correlates more directly with
"the state of the union" than with the
state of relations between Britain and the
Catholic powers on the Continent. Every
domestic crisis, for some reason, brought

[2] *The Development of Religious Toleration in
England* by W. K. Jordan, 1932, Vol. I, p. 162.

[3] *Ibid.*, Vol. II, pp. 7 and 157; Vol. III, p. 17.

forth new "revelations" about the papists or yet another artfully rigged "incident."

Today the verbalisms by which this incessant persecution of the Catholic minority was justified have a familiar sound. For example, in his famous "Apologie for the Oath of Allegiance," King James insisted that the anti-Catholic measures were purely civil and precautionary; he was concerned with the "loyalty," not the beliefs, of Catholics. It was his purpose to distinguish between "loyal" and "disloyal" Catholics, or, as he put it, between "trew subjects" and "false-hearted traitors." The oath was simply a device by which the former could be distinguished from the latter; no offense was intended. "No man hath lost his life," he explained, "no man hath indured the racke, no man hath suffered corporall punishment in other kinds, meerely or simply, or in any degree or respect, for his conscience in matter of religion." Yet all these things *were* happening to Catholics and the situation kept getting worse. No matter how often or how thoroughly the loyal Catholics were sorted out from the disloyal, the process was repeated with each new crisis in domestic affairs. The severity of the measures, also, seemed to increase with the gravity of the domestic crisis.

The test oath, of course, was the principal instrument by which Catholics were identified. Ostensibly concerned with loyalty, it was really an instrument used in a struggle for power between partisan groups. For years the best legal minds in England kept tinkering with the oath, clause by clause, word by word, until it finally became, in the words of Sir Frederick Pollock, "swollen with strange imprecations and scoldings." Every word in the oath was intended to make it that much more difficult for Catholics to challenge the dominance of Protestants, al-though the oath was always justified in terms of the "foreign danger" and "the Jesuit problem." Not only did the oath taker pledge allegiance and agree to respect the line of succession but he was also required to repudiate any foreign allegiance and to abjure specific Catholic doctrines. This "doctrinal disavowal" was supposed to make the oath papist-proof; to make it airtight. No emphasis is required to point up the extraordinary power which the test oath gave to those who did the "testing" over those who were being "tested."

Once imposed, the test oath became increasingly vexatious as more abjurations and disavowals were constantly added and the penalties for perjury were increased. But the basic objection always went, not to the form of the oath, but to the very idea that a majority should arrogate to itself such a tyrannical power to intimidate and coerce a minority. Furthermore, the test oath imposed a definite qualification upon the rights of citizens; in fact it made citizenship a revocable privilege. As the author of a tract published in 1678 pointed out, the test oath destroyed the natural rights of the peerage and "turned the birthright of the English nobility into a precarious title. . . . What was in all former Ages only forfeited by Treason is now at the mercy of every Faction or every Passion in Parliament." Yet then as now the test oath was defended as an innocent expression of patriotic sentiment. No loyal American, we are told, could possibly object to making an affirmation of loyalty in which various foreign allegiances and "subversive" doctrines are repudiated. But if circumstances require an affirmation of loyalty, they will also require investigation and surveillance. And any attempt to investigate or verify the affirmation presupposes the use of spies and informers, the services of a political police, and the existence of some Star Chamber before which suspects can be haled for questioning. It also implies disabilities and penalties other than sentences for perjury. Thus a procedure originally sanctioned as a "mere ceremony" suddenly turns out to be a means by which some citizens impose disabilities on other citizens without due process of law.

Measures for testing loyalty are invariably developed outside the existing legal framework. Like other crisis-inspired measures, they are defended as temporary devices improvised to meet a special emergency. It seems entirely proper, therefore, to tolerate certain departures from traditional forms. Besides, the fiction prevails that to charge a person with being disloyal is not to charge him with the commission of a criminal offense. Today, for example, the meanest pickpocket in the land can demand, as a matter of right, the protection of constitutional safeguards which government employees with long records of faithful service are denied by the loyalty review boards. The purpose of loyalty testing, it is said, is not to punish anyone — perish the thought! — but to guard the nation's security. As Macaulay caustically observed: "Only a rank Jacobite and an enemy of the Whig Party" would dare contend that the test oath had criminal overtones or that it resembled an ex post facto indictment. The difficulty, of course, is that the security of a nation is indistinguishable from the security of its citizens in the exercise of their rights. . . .

The Dual Conflict

None of the parties to the incredibly bitter "religious wars" seemed to realize that the fanaticism of faith clearly masked a fanaticism of avarice. The trag-

edy of the situation, as Tawney pointed out, consisted in the fact that the problems of a swiftly changing economic environment should have burst on Europe at a time when it was already torn by religious dissension.[4] These problems were naturally debated in terms of religious partisanship; but differences in social theory did not coincide with differences in religious affiliation. The struggle was not between capitalist Protestants and Catholic guildsmen but between producers and merchants some of whom were Catholics and some of whom were Protestants. The economic revolution prolonged and greatly intensified the religious controversy by vastly augmenting the stakes for which the parties contended. Conversely, the religious division made it possible to organize the struggle for control and dominance of the new social forces released by the economic revolution. "Anti-Catholicism" in England was, so to speak, the principle upon which social power was organized and, as such, it naturally had to be stepped up whenever a domestic crisis threatened the existing social controls. By providing a basis and rationale for exclusion, it gave a specific direction to the struggle for place and position.

Today an economic revolution, resembling that which swept over Europe during the "religious wars," cuts across national conflicts in much the same manner that the economic revolution of that period cut across religious dissensions. The fact that national rivalries, for all practical purposes, have been reduced to the rivalry between two great powers merely underscores the parallel. The revival of commodity production at the end of the Middle Ages did not cause so much as it exacerbated the religious con-

---

[4] *Religion and the Rise of Capitalism* by R. H. Tawney, 1926, p. 82.

flict between Catholic and Protestant; and, similarly, the economic revolution of our time has not caused so much as it has intensified, and greatly complicated, national rivalries. Now as then the world is caught in a dual conflict: economic-theological then, economic-ideological now. Increasingly the great power rivalry of our time tends to be transformed into a world-wide ideological conflict. When a concern is expressed today over a person's "loyalty," as often as not it is his "ideological" loyalty which is in doubt; but unfortunately neither ideological nor religious loyalties respect national boundaries. In our time two conflicts, by no means identical (Socialism is not identical with Russian nationalism), have tended to fuse and the obsession with loyalty reflects this confusion. Thus we brand the ideological nonconformist as "disloyal" just as, in the period of the "religious wars," the religious nonconformist was persecuted as "an enemy" of the state in which he had been born, whose language was the only language he knew, and beyond whose borders he had probably never traveled.

It will be objected that the parallel with the "religious wars" is too remote; that the historical background of the test oath has no relevance to "the problem of Communism." But just where did the test oath first reappear in modern times? Oddly enough in Nazi Germany and Fascist Italy where police terror had reduced the idea of an oath to utter absurdity. In reviving the test oath, the Nazis were not quaintly attempting to test loyalty by medieval standards; they used the oath to humiliate and destroy political opponents. For example, there were any number of men in the German and Italian universities who were known as antifascists. But once these men had been compelled to take the oath of loyalty, they were morally discredited in the eyes of all who knew them and, more important, in their own eyes as well. Every antifascist who took the oath by this very fact undermined respect for the values upon which the opposition to fascism rested. With the Nazis and Fascists, the test oath was clearly a means by which political opponents were silenced and discredited and not a means by which loyalty was tested. Such an astute terrorist as Dr. Goebbels would have placed slight credence in an affirmation of loyalty from a German with an antifascist record; he understood the dual conflict of our times too well for that.

The failure to appreciate the meaning of test oaths is based in part upon a failure to recognize that dictatorships are brought into being by social conditions and not by evil notions or dangerous thoughts. Dictatorships appear during periods of maladjustment, when, as Dr. William Yale has pointed out, "the unity of the social group is torn to shreds by the variety of suffering and the resulting diversity of discontents."[5] The maladjustment is usually related to an inability to control the environment which comes about either through an ability to produce more than the society can consume at a profit or from an inability to produce all that is needed. Whatever the cause, social institutions do not lose their validity until they have ceased to be suitable adjustments. When the maladjustment becomes acute and chronic, the resulting instability is said to be the work of "termites" and "fifth columnists" and the test oath and similar loyalty devices are then demanded as means by which "disloyal" elements can be identified. Instead of investigating causes, the society persecutes heretics; instead of unearthing reasons, it

[5] *Journal of Social Psychology*, July 1939, pp. 336–340.

undertakes to suppress criticism. "It is distressing to realize," writes Dr. Carl J. Friedrich, "that the oath has always cropped up as a political device when the political order was crumbling. In the period of religious dissensions, the oath of allegiance made its appearance in England as an instrument of intolerance and, a little later, of royal aggression."[6]

"The Censorious Eye"

In the main, we, the American people, have misjudged the motivation of the loyalty program because we have forgotten that the loyalty obsession really began twenty-five years ago, when the Soviet Union was merely an international hypothesis. It was during and immediately after World War I that loyalty first became a major obsession with us and, then as now, a special concern was voiced over the loyalty of teachers. The frenzy of these years culminated in the passage of the Lusk Laws in New York in 1921. From the day of their adoption, the laws involved the administration of the schools in a nightmare of dissension, litigation, and confusion. An orgy of investigation and harassment took place as individuals squared away to settle personal grievances and disputes that had been accumulating for decades. "Principals, supervisors, fellow-teachers," writes Dr. Howard K. Beale, "were now free to report for trial for 'disloyalty' and for possible dismissal any teachers against whom they had grievances."[7] The mere threat of investigation proved to be quite sufficient to frighten teachers into a blind conformity. Indeed "the censorious eye" was more effective, according to Dr. Beale, than actual force or coercion because "dismissals would have raised pro-

tests whereas terrorization gained its end without unpleasant publicity."

Ironically the power of the Soviet Union to seduce rather than subvert the American people was then given as the main justification for the concern with loyalty. No one dreamed of suggesting at that time that the Soviet Union actually menaced the national security of the United States. Writing in opposition to the Lusk Laws, John Dewey shrewdly observed that the laws were "only the *outward symbol* of that tendency on the part of big business in our present economic society to hold teachers within definite prescribed limits. These suppressive tendencies work in a more refined way than laws. The great body of teachers are unaware of their existence. They are felt only through little hints about 'safety,' 'sanity,' and 'sobriety' coming from influential sources. . . . It is something more than academic freedom that is being menaced. It is moral freedom, the right to think, to imagine. It involves, when it is crushed, a crushing of all that is best in the way of inspiration and ideals for a better order."[8]

The existence of a *real* external enemy does not provoke the type of fear which appears in loyalty obsessions. Fear in the presence of a real enemy can be exhilarating. The fear that found expression in the Lusk Laws was a morbid fear of self; a fear of the people as reflected in the group thinking of a dominant class. It should be emphasized that the "Bolshevism" against which reaction inveighed in 1919–1922 was, to most people, the vaguest of doctrines. There was no network of Communist parties through the world then nor was Russia the great power it is today. Nevertheless Bolshevism was denounced with the same vehe-

[6] "Teachers' Oaths," *Harper's*, January 1936, pp. 171–177.

[7] *Are American Teachers Free?* 1936.

[8] Quoted by Beale, p. 571.

mence that Communism is denounced today. In further confirmation of John Dewey's theory, it might be pointed out that the nation's concern with loyalty did not reach the intensity of an obsession until immediately *after* World War I. Reaction never has too much to fear when the people are engaged in a war, when armies have been mobilized, and when special wartime powers and controls have been invoked. But the moment "peace breaks out," loyalty becomes a problem.

As a matter of fact the "menace" in the period from 1919 to 1922 was Socialism rather than Bolshevism. The New York Council on Education then found that "membership in the Socialist Party was incompatible with the obligations of the teaching profession." Legislative committees made findings that the Socialist Party was "not a party in the usual sense," exactly paralleling current findings about the Communist Party. Five members of the Socialist Party were summarily expelled from the New York Legislature for being "disloyal" and Congress refused to seat Victor Berger, the Socialist, who had been elected from the Fifth Congressional District of Wisconsin. In 1919 three prominent Socialists, all anti-Communists today, as they were then, were dismissed as teachers from the New York schools. In all this excitement, one can look in vain for even a suggestion that the Soviet Union, as such, menaced the security of the United States in the sense in which that "menace" is expressed today.

Once the nation had returned to "normalcy" following the severe deflation of the postwar period, the obsession with loyalty quickly abated despite the fact that it had become apparent, by then, that the Soviet Union would survive and that it was rapidly consolidating its posi-

tion. But with "everything under control," with the sun of the Coolidge prosperity upon the land, the menace of Socialism became merely the memory of an ugly nightmare. However, in line with the Dewey thesis, the tendency to repress all criticism did not entirely disappear. A number of organizations continued to agitate for a general loyalty program as a permanent part of the structure of government. Then, in 1934, the Hearst press launched a new campaign against "radicals" in the schools and colleges. It was in this same year also that the campaign to require the flag salute in the school was launched, all as part of a drive for "patriotic conformity." Within five years, some fourteen states had adopted laws requiring teachers to take loyalty oaths.

Today it is generally agreed that the emphasis on loyalty in this campaign of 1934–1935 was primarily occasioned by the fear of the early reforms of the New Deal and, more particularly, by the approaching 1936 election. It should be noted that the Soviet Union had been recognized by the United States before the campaign was launched and that this, generally, was the period of the popular front and of Litvinoff's stirring speeches in favor of collective security. One can say that the Soviet Union was not in any sense then regarded as a "national enemy." Here, again, is striking proof that John Dewey had correctly analyzed the Lusk Laws as a manifestation of a more or less constant trend in the society. Seen in the perspective of a quarter century, it is clear that our current obsession with loyalty, like the similar obsession in the Soviet Union, is influenced by, but not caused by, the state of relations between the two countries.

That internal tensions provide the real motivation for loyalty campaigns becomes clear the moment one examines, not the national loyalty program, but its local counterparts. For example, on April 1, 1947, the Board of Supervisors of Los Angeles, following the lead of President Truman, and never to be left behind in any crusade, adopted a loyalty program based on a test oath containing specific disavowals. During the war, not a single case of disloyalty had been reported among the county's 20,000 employees; yet, with substantially the same employees on the payroll, the county suddenly became concerned with their loyalty two years after the war was over. In this case, the loyalty ordinance was clearly adopted as part of a drive for political conformity; it had nothing to do with "security." Officials who wanted to vote against the proposal told me that they feared to oppose it. Newspaper editors hesitated to criticize the proposal although frankly conceding its absurdity. Influential citizens privately confessed their misgivings but were reluctant to voice a protest. The security equation was not changed in the slightest degree by the adoption of the ordinance but the campaign to secure its adoption, and its adoption, undeniably coerced opinion, and made for conformity.

Footnote to History

Perhaps a footnote to history may help to explain the nature of loyalty obsessions . . .

The first response to the French Revolution in the United States was one of elation, sympathy, and popular support. As the revolution swept forward, however, this initial support narrowed down and became increasingly partisan. The more the struggle in France was debated, the more its domestic implications were emphasized. Democratic Clubs sprang up on all sides to support the revolution, and also to discuss domestic political

questions. "Meeting regularly through the year," to quote Claude G. Bowers, "they were teaching the mechanic, the clerk, the small farmer, to think in terms of politics."[9] The Federalists, out to monopolize power in the wake of national liberation, promptly denounced the clubs as "demoniacal societies" and "nurseries of sedition" which should be suppressed at the earliest opportunity. To create such an opportunity, they began to develop the thesis that the French Revolution imperiled American interests; therefore, all those who supported the French were per se "subversive" and a menace to the Federalist Party. But the formula also worked just as well in reverse: anyone who agitated for social reform and opposed the Federalist Party was, by this token, pro-French and therefore "disloyal."

By the time Adams was inaugurated as President, popular enthusiasm for the revolution had noticeably abated. This could only mean that the danger of domestic, native "subversion" had declined and, with this decline, one would naturally have expected that the danger of a war with France would have tapered off. But the powerful Hamiltonian wing of the Federalist Party promptly seized this moment to demand a declaration of war, seeking by this agitation to weaken still further the movement for social reform. "The French Stamp," with which they began to smear their opponents, was simply a partisan tactic in this campaign. Curiously enough, the louder the war party clamored for a war against the French (who were "menacing" American interests), the more violently they denounced, not the French, but their political opponents in America.

To climax this campaign, and to de-

[9] *Jefferson and Hamilton: The Struggle for Democracy in America*, 1925, p. 256.

stroy the Democratic Clubs, which were more concerned with domestic than with international politics, the Federalists pushed through the Alien and Sedition Acts. The Alien Act was primarily aimed not at the French, but at the Irish. If the Irish had been conservatives, their sympathy with the French might have been overlooked; but as followers of Jefferson it was clear that they should be summarily deported. The Federalists even tried to make it appear that the Irish were guilty of a plot to overthrow the government. On the other hand, the clear purpose of the Sedition Act was "to crush the opposition press and silence criticism of the ruling powers," all in the guise of protecting America against subversive French ideas and an Irish fifth column. Advocated as part of a drive for war against a "foreign enemy," the act was aimed not at this enemy, but at the American people. Ironically both bills were debated, as Bowers put it, "under conditions of disorder that would have disgraced a discussion of brigands wrangling over a division of spoils in a wayside cave." The Federalists — those apostles of "law and order," those enemies of "French anarchy"— hooted and howled, scraped their feet, coughed, laughed; and resorted to physical violence in an effort to intimidate their opponents in debate. In a magnificent speech against the Alien Bill, Edward Livingston vividly foretold how the act would be used and what effects it would have:

The country will swarm with informers, spies, relators, and all the odious reptile tribe that breed in the sunshine of despotic power. ... The hours of the most unsuspected confidence, the intimacies of friendship, or the recesses of domestic retirement, afford no security. The companion whom you must trust, the friend in whom you must confide, the domestic who waits in your chamber, are all tempted to betray your imprudent or unguarded follies; to misrepresent your words; to convey them, distorted by calumny, to the secret tribunal where jealousy presides — where fear officiates as accuser, and suspicion is the only evidence that is heard. ... Do not let us be told that we are to excite a fervor against a foreign aggression to establish a tyranny at home; that like the arch traitor we cry "Hail Columbia" at the moment we are betraying her to destruction; that we sing, "Happy Land," when we are plunging it in ruin and disgrace; and that we are absurd enough to call ourselves free and enlightened while we advocate principles that would have disgraced the age of Gothic barbarity.

With the passage of the Alien and Sedition Acts, a Reign of Terror broke upon the land which, beginning in 1798, extended through the autumn of 1800. Then as now, the press, the clergy, the colleges, all joined in the great crusade to coerce total conformity as the prelude to a declaration of war. Mobs broke into the headquarters of the Democratic Clubs. Artisans employed in the manufacture of war materials were driven from their jobs with charges of being "pro-French" and "disloyal." Newspapers screamed that any person who doubted the wisdom of either the Alien or the Sedition Act deserved to be listed as disloyal, and the Right Reverend Bishop White of Philadelphia announced that those who opposed either measure "resisteth the ordinance of God." Hamilton was commissioned a major general; the harbor of New York was fortified; and a campaign was launched to recruit a large standing army. Editors were arrested and convicted under the Sedition Act; Congressmen were threatened with arrest for the offense of writing letters to their constituents; and lawyers who defended those charged with sedition were denounced from the bench for "propagating dangerous principles." From 1798 to 1801, liberty, as Bowers wrote, "was mobbed in America."

Every effort was made by the war party, of course, to prevent President Adams from sending commissioners to negotiate a treaty with the French and the situation in France was consistently misrepresented in the American press. Federalist editors did not hesitate to develop the theme that a war with France would be a good business for the struggling colonies. Hamilton kept assuring the President that the Bourbons would soon be restored by the coalition and that it would be folly to seek a treaty with the French government then in power. But once the commissioners had sailed, the ground was suddenly cut from beneath the war party and, with Jefferson's election, the loyalty obsession quickly abated. The new President refused to prosecute those arrested before the Sedition Act expired on March 3, 1801, pardoned those who had been convicted and were still in jail, and ultimately Congress repaid most of the fines levied under the act. The sudden disappearance of the loyalty obsession *once the opposition had come to power* is striking evidence that domestic politics had more to do with this obsession than foreign loyalties or European politics.

The pattern in England was similar although the end result was quite different. The British, too, had greeted the revolution with enthusiasm. But with the publication of Burke's *Reflections* in 1790, the first tonic enthusiasm was soon displaced by a wave of fear and hostility which, set in motion by the upper classes, finally spread throughout the nation. . . .

The entire movement for social reform in Britain was stigmatized as "disloyal" through the simple stratagem of calling attention to the fact that most of the reformers were, or had been, sympathetic to the French Revolution. This made them, of course, "agents of a foreign power," and thereby convicted a lot of them of "constructive treason." The net result was to make any and every aspect of social reform synonymous with treason. Literally all reform measures, "mild, moderate and extreme," were alike tarred as disloyal and subversive. Wilberforce, who had asked leave in 1790 to bring in a bill to bar the traffic in slaves, suddenly discovered that the bill had become "pro-French" and subversive. Then, as in our time, important intellectuals, like Coleridge, Wordsworth, and Southey, ingloriously recanted, "went over to the government," and sought injunctions in the courts when Leigh Hunt and Hazlitt, with a fine sense of mischief, began to reprint their earlier "odes to freedom." . . .

However we may read this footnote to history, we should be able to agree on this: that the brutalization of the intellectual, social, and political life of *a society*, that is, of a people united by common bonds of culture and tradition, of language and history, is a crime of a magnitude that cannot be readily measured. The crushing of the reform movement in Britain may have been a partisan victory for the Tories but it was truly a national disaster. The extent of this disaster can only be appreciated by contrasting the condition of the British working class, in the decades after 1800, with the remarkable advances made by the American working class which, thanks largely to Jefferson's leadership, had succeeded in upsetting the Federalist counterpart of the Tory plot. Heresy hunts have the effect of draining off vital group energies which any society must accumulate if it is to solve the problems of survival. To spread fear and suspicion *within a society* is to poison the life of that society at its source, which is to be found in the ability of the people to cooperate. There can never be a satisfactory excuse or justification for this particular crime. If the danger from abroad is real, then all the more reason why unity should be fostered among the people, and the greater the danger, the greater the need for unity. Given the right combination of circumstances, it is easy to launch a heresy hunt — as easy as it is to squeeze the trigger of a gun. But the consequences are likely to reverberate long after the echo of the shot has died away. . . .

Heresy Hunting Is Not Scapegoating

Just as heresy is to be distinguished from dissent, so heresy hunting is not synonymous with scapegoating. Scapegoating is universal and perennial; it is based on the simplest form of delusion. Witch hunting is a form of social madness based on delusions which are paranoid. Scapegoating is largely an individual phenomenon; witch hunting is a product of collective madness. The key to the distinction is to be found in the fact that scapegoating may be stimulated by mild frustration but witch hunting stems only from major social dislocations. Witch hunting, as Marion L. Starkey has pointed out, always comes "in the wake of stress and social disorganization"; after wars, disasters, plagues, famines, and revolutions. Scapegoating appears in all seasons; but witch hunting only reappears in time of storm. The nature of witch hunts as such, the manner in which they unfold, and the dynamics which they set in motion, form an important chapter in the sociology of heresy.

The psychology of the witch trail is the psychology of the un-American investigation. Witches will lie; so will Communists. Witches get innocent people to do their bidding; so do Communists. One can be a witch without knowing it just as one can be a Communist without knowing it. Witches were convicted on "spectral" evidence and today a "spectral" use is made of the doctrine of guilt by association. Abigail Williams, whose fantasies damned the innocent in Salem in 1691, can be identified today as a fairly obvious psychological type; but even the wise, intelligent, and honest Samuel Sewall was taken in, at the time, by the antics of Abigail. And so today, equally wise and honest men seem quite incapable of detecting the element of fantasy and delusion which appears in the neurotically embroidered tales of Abigail's modern counterparts, whose passion for truth and patriotism is reborn simultaneously with the disappearance of their fifth column lovers.

Major social dislocations seem to produce a kind of social hallucination which makes it possible for simple delusions, based on a failure to understand the psychology of chance, to go undetected even by ordinarily astute minds. For example: the Polish Ambassador holds a reception; the wife of a scientist is invited; at the reception she meets X, the so-called Soviet agent. A product of pure chance, this meeting is put down, in time of storm, as evidence of a conspiracy. It is the same delusion, however, which once caused people to believe that because the farmer's cow died the day Goody Jenkins walked through the barnyard, therefore Goody Jenkins, the witch, killed the cow. For in a time of storm the line which divides fact from fantasy breaks down or becomes hopelessly blurred and shifting. Delusions that would be spotted immediately in normal times can then pass as the most self-evident and uncontestable realities. In such periods coincidence looms larger than logic and life-long reputations can be toppled over by a whisper of suspicion launched by an anonymous informer.

Before social disorganization can produce a witch hunt, however, a well-organized system of police terror must be in existence. It is this factor which calls forth the mania of denunciation which is so characteristic of witch hunts. The motives for denunciation are usually mixed — fanaticism, the conforming tendency, covetousness, fear — but it is police terror which directly inspires the mania. The susceptibility of the Germans to the form of witch hunt launched by the Nazis is to be explained by the fact that a long acquaintance with the methods of a political police, and a long political police tradition, had bred in many Germans a passion for conformity. In all terroristic regimes, as Bramstedt points out, ". . . the accused is everybody outside the limited circle of privileged organizations and the ruling clique"; therefore, those outside this limited circle must constantly prove, by words and deed, and principally by denunciations, that they are loyal. The mania of denunciation springs not from the fear of heretics but from a well-founded and quite realistic fear of the machinery which has been set up to catch heretics.

Although this heresy-catching machinery provides an ingenious form of social control, it has distinct limitations. For one thing, the price to be paid for the suppression of heresies in terms of what it will purchase is clearly prohibitive. If we were to enact every measure proposed by the anti-Communists for the suppression of Communism we would find that we had destroyed the fabric of civil rights and that the number of Communists would probably be the same or greater today! The self-defeating char-

acter of the anti-Communist strategy is reflected in the headline of a story by W. H. Lawrence in the *New York Times* of January 2, 1950: "Brazil Reds Busy, Though Outlawed." Outlawed three years previously, the Communists of Brazil, Mr. Lawrence discovered, were more numerous and more active than ever. Thus those who favor measures to suppress heresy must be made to carry a dual burden of proof. They must be made to prove: (1) that the dangers are "clear and present"; and (2) that repressive measures will actually guard against these dangers. It is on the second point that their case invariably breaks down.

Not only are heresy hunts expensive in terms of what they will actually accomplish, but they involve a peculiar law of diminishing returns. At first, only the vulnerable, the easily "fingered" victims are selected. For example, the first witches arrested in Salem were an illiterate slave, an old crone, and a lascivious grandmother. Carting these victims off to the gallows aroused little opposition; indeed it fanned the flames of intolerance. But heresy hunts must be kept going; new victims must be found. The second batch of victims will be less vulnerable than the first but their immolation will not arouse much protest either because these victims are usually unpopular, poor, and lacking in social prestige. By this time, however, the informers, inquisitors, and psychopathic witnesses have become drunk with the new-found power of denunciation. They begin to enjoy the notoriety that goes with being an expert on witchcraft and a professional "denouncer"; they thrill to the feeling of being able to destroy another person by merely voicing a phrase, or pointing a finger, or whispering an accusation.

As the accusers become bolder, the

range of accusation broadens and "heresy" ceases to have any definable meaning. Individuals are now haled before the tribunal who have real roots in the community, who are generally liked and respected. Doubts then begin to arise, for the first time, that the informers are truthful, doubts which never arose when the victims were marginal types. But by this time the machinery of persecution cannot be stopped, much less reversed. To admit error would be to cast doubt on the prior convictions and to undermine the concept of heresy. The informers, during this second act, usually become frightened of the consequences of their perjuries, and the more frightened they become, the bolder their accusations, the wilder their denunciations. Informers then begin to inform on informers in an effort to prevent any possible betrayal of their fraudulent charges and counterfeit "revelations." By this time, too, the power of denunciation has become truly frightening. A destructive self-hatred then exists in the society, like the fumes of an explosive gas, that anyone can ignite by merely striking a match. Sooner or later, however, the list of "expendable" victims must be exhausted, and at this point society recoils from the excesses of witch hunting, in weariness and horror. "Sound" elements, silent all this while, then step forward to exert a moderating influence, and gradually, slowly, like a patient recovering from a long fever, with its attendant hallucinations, society begins to recover its sanity and health.

But sanity does not always return; sometimes the society destroys itself, for the cost of eradicating heresy is in direct proportion to the success of the operation. Who would care to estimate the price paid for the Salem persecutions? Nor should it be forgotten that Spain was the one nation in which the Inquisition was really successful and the price, there, was intellectual ruin and political and moral decay. Once society starts burning heretics, figuratively or literally, the flames are likely to engulf the whole structure of society. Thus the basic reason why heresy persecutions are futile is the risk that they might succeed and the price of success is utter ruin.

Arthur M. Schlesinger, Jr.:

WHAT IS LOYALTY? A DIFFICULT QUESTION

WE have heard a good deal in recent months about loyalty and Americanism. Spokesmen on one side proclaim that the American way of life is in imminent danger from any one who questions the eternal rightness of the capitalist system. Spokesmen on the other side proclaim that a sinister witch-hunt is already transforming the United States into a totalitarian police state.

The situation cries out for a little less hysteria and a little more calm sense. A

Reprinted from *The New York Times Magazine,* November 2, 1947. Used by permission.

calm survey surely reveals two proposi-
tions on which we can all agree: (1) that
Americanism is not a totalitarian faith,
which can impose a single economic or
political dogma or require a uniformity
in observance from all its devotees; but
(2) that a serious problem for national
security has been created by that fanati-
cal group which rejects all American interests in favor of those of the Soviet
Union.

In other words, the disciples of the Un-
American Activities Committee and the
leadership of the American Legion must
be reminded that Americanism means
something far richer and deeper than
submission to their own collection of
petty prejudices; and civil libertarians
who honestly fear a witch-hunt must be
reminded that in an imperfect world of
spies and traitors a Government must be
conceded the right of self-protection. We
see here an inescapable conflict between
civil liberty and national security, and
we must face up to the problem of resolv-
ing the conflict.

What is Americanism? To get quickly
to what its loudest exponents seem to
regard as its basic point — private enterprise — there is nothing un-American
about criticizing the capitalist system.
Let us reveal the hideous secret: capitalism was not handed down with the Ten
Commandments at Sinai. The Constitution of the United States does not ordain
the economic status quo. It can well be
argued that there is nothing in our fundamental law to prevent Congress from
socializing all basic industry tomorrow:
there is certainly nothing in our state
laws to prevent public ownership.

Are we to assume that revelations concerning the sacrosanctity of private capitalism have been vouchsafed to the NAM
and to the Republican party which were
denied to the Founding Fathers? More

than this, the basic tradition in American democracy — the tradition associated
with such names as Jefferson, Jackson,
Wilson and the two Roosevelts — has
been a fight on behalf of the broad
masses against the economic excesses of
capitalism and against the political aspi-
rations of the business community.

It is even hard to argue that assertion
of the right of revolution is un-American.
According to that once-respected document, the Declaration of Independence,
when a government becomes injurious to
life, liberty and the pursuit of happiness,
"it is the right of the people to alter or
to abolish it and to institute new government, laying its foundation on such principles and organizing its power in such
form as to them shall seem most likely
to effect their safety and happiness."

James Wilson, one of the fathers of
the Constitution and perhaps a greater
authority on it than the chairman of the
Un-American Activities Committee, declared: "A revolution principle certainly
is, and certainly should be taught as a
principle of the Constitution of the
United States." Surely no one like Congressman Rankin, who holds Gen. Robert
E. Lee and his colleagues in pious vener-
ation, has much ground for stickling at
the thought of armed rebellion.

This insistence on the infallibility of
capitalism and on the heresy of change
finds no sanction in the usages of the
American democratic tradition. It reaches
its pinnacle of imbecility in such epi-
sodes as the attack on the film "The Best
Years of Our Lives" as Communist-
minded because it makes fun of the
American business man, or in the standards employed by the Un-American
Committee in their current Hollywood
investigation. What havoc the rigid identification of Americanism with business
worship would wreak upon the history

and traditions of our country! Yet this very identification pervades altogether too much of the popular campaign against communism. Many conservatives are happily pouncing upon the Communist scare as an excuse for silencing all critics of business supremacy.

But those who believe that the agitation over communism is only a pretext for purging liberals — that this is a repetition of A. Mitchell Palmer and the red raids — are themselves mistaking a part for the whole. Times have changed a good deal since A. Mitchell Palmer. In 1919 the U.S.S.R. was a torn and struggling nation with its back to the wall. Today Soviet totalitarianism is massive, well-organized and on the march. Its spies and agents are ubiquitous. We face here not just a figment of the reactionary imagination but a proved problem for the security of free nations.

Experience by now must have exposed the illusion that it is possible to work with Communists or fellow-travelers — with persons whose loyalties are signed, sealed and delivered elsewhere. President Gonzales Videla of Chile and Joe Curran of the National Maritime Union have presented only the most recent case histories. One may still wonder perhaps whether the divergence of political loyalties really goes to the length of espionage. Again the record is clear. Herbert Morrison, hardly a reactionary, has borne testimony, for example, to the cases of Communist espionage which came to him as British Home Secretary at a time when Britain and Russia were fighting allies.

"It may be said that all countries spy, and it may be that they do," Morrison observed. "But there is a grave difference between the ordinary spying of the professional spy . . . and espionage through a political organization." The documents of the Canadian spy case report the techniques of Communist political corruption in fascinating and indisputable detail — in particular, the use of the "study group" as a way of feeling out the degrees of political fanaticism.

The national Communist parties and their front organizations provide, in fact, a unique means of getting, recruiting and testing potential agents. Morrison has stated one result of these tactics — his discomfort at the thought of "sitting in the same cabinet where members of the American Communist party were participating in our discussions with access to secret documents." That discomfort must continue wherever in government agencies, Communists or their allies or dupes have access to classified materials.

It would be rash to assume that Moscow has its intelligence networks operating in every country except the one it has repeatedly named as its chief enemy — the United States. Certainly the American Communist party has made no secret of its belief that the United States should always follow the Soviet lead. As recently as September, 1947, *Political Affairs*, the American Communist theological organ, made its usual references to the "fact" that "the policies of the Soviet Union before, during and since the anti-Axis war, have corresponded to the best interests of the American people."

In view of such repeated declarations, it becomes increasingly difficult to see how even Henry Wallace can continue saying, "The very few Communists I have met have been very good Americans." The presumption becomes overwhelming that the U.S.S.R., through the NKVD, its underground Communist cells and its front organizations, is commissioning agents to penetrate the "sensitive" branches of the Government, particularly the State Department, the Department of National Defense and the Atomic Energy Commission.

Let us then admit that a real danger exists. But the solution is surely not, on the one hand, to fire every one suspected of liberal leanings, nor, on the other, to fire only avowed and open Communists. The solution is rather to construct some means of ridding the security agencies of questionable characters, while at the same time retaining enough safeguards to insure against indiscriminate purges.

Discharge in advance of an overt act may seem a rough policy. Yet the failure to discharge suspicious persons may well imperil national security; it certainly would lead to the use of precautionary measures, such as wire-tapping and constant shadowing, which would bring the police state much nearer. Let us recall for a moment the situation in 1938. Obviously Nazis, their conscious fellow-travelers and soft-headed Americans who conceived Germany to be a much misunderstood nation had no business in the State Department; and liberals were correct in demanding their dismissal in advance of overt acts. I cannot see why this same principle does not apply today to the fellow-travelers of a rival totalitarianism.

Have we, in fact, a witch-hunt today? We must first discriminate between the wishes of some members of Congress and the intentions of the Executive. The most shocking actions of the Administration — notably the President's executive order, the State Department's loyalty code and some of the recent firings — have doubtless been motivated in great part by a desire to head off more extreme action from Congress. Yet this very process of appeasing the worst element in Congress has led to the compromise of principles which cannot be properly compromised

in a democracy. Appeasement has produced throughout the Executive Branch an atmosphere of apprehension and anxiety that is fatal to boldness in government.

We may agree that this picture can be overdrawn — that Communist propaganda in this country is working overtime to paint Washington as a terror-ridden police state. Presumably on the basis of such overwrought stories, Harold Laski can write in *The New Statesman* and *Nation,* "America is in the grip of an hysterical witch-hunt that is as ugly in its character as it is fantastic in its proportions." We can only admire the effectiveness of the propaganda campaign. Indeed, one atrocity story went so far in claiming that all readers of liberal magazines would fall under suspicion that the rumor boomeranged in the shape of cancellations flowing into the magazine offices.

The New Republic then made haste to state editorially, as it had not bothered to do before, that the subscribers were unnecessarily agitated and were only victims of "the new war of nerves. Both the Civil Service Commission and the Federal Bureau of Investigation, the two agencies that probe the loyalty of Federal employes, flatly deny asking questions about the reading habits of government employes."

Yet the executive order and the State Department code are inexcusably defective. In particular, the recent action of the State Department in denying most of those discharged both the right to a hearing and the right to resignation without prejudice betrays a state of mind going beyond the requirements of security and entering the realm of persecution. The department must be able to terminate employment on suspicion; this can be done in a number of ways; but the department cannot be allowed to stigmatize individuals and wreck lives on suspicion.

One may understand the travail of people trying to frame security regulations with the hot breath of Parnell Thomas and John Rankin on their necks; but the results go too far in waiving traditional procedural guarantees. The final result can only be to enthrone the narrow, bureaucratic conformist at the expense of the courageous and independent public servant — and at the ultimate expense of the belief in human dignity which purports to be the main objective of our foreign policy.

Still, honest civil libertarians might better devote themselves, not to blanket abuse of any attempts to meet the problem but to the construction of alternatives which would better secure individual rights while still permitting the Government to deal effectively with the grim dangers of foreign espionage. As Herbert Morrison once said, "It is easier to criticize Governments fighting this business of espionage than to be that Government that has to fight the espionage." . . .

The press has an equal responsibility, for the final safeguard against injustice lies in the appeal to public opinion. *The Washington Post,* for example, has done a notable job in the nation's capital in guarding against the violation of civil liberties. In this connection it is interesting to note that, except for the courageous Miss Yuhas, none of the victims of the alleged reign of terror in the State Department has yet availed himself of the opportunities proffered to set forth his case in the press.

The situation imposes a special responsibility, too, I think, upon the American left. Liberals who complain when Parnell Thomas fails to distinguish between liberals and Communists should remember that too often they have failed to make that distinction themselves. History by now has surely documented that distinction to the point of surfeit; the attack on the free Socialist parties in the recent Belgrade manifesto is only the most recent example of the deadly Soviet hostility to the non-Communist left.

The liberal movement in this country must reject the Communists as forthrightly as the British Labor party has rejected them; it must not squander its energy and influence in covering up for them. This is the dictate of strategy as well as principle. Whatever conservatism may say about Wilson Wyatt or Leon Henderson and Americans for Democratic Action, or about such labor leaders as Walter Reuther and David Dubinsky, it cannot combat them by smearing them as fellow-travelers.

But the situation imposes just as grave a responsibility upon American conservatives. They must remember that the only criterion for disloyalty is superior loyalty to another country, and that reservations about the capitalist system or skepticism concerning the wisdom of the business community are by themselves no evidence at all of external loyalties. The essential fight in Europe today, for example, is between socialism and communism; and socialism has many supporters and sympathizers in this country who are resolutely anti-totalitarian. If the leadership of this country were to be confined to men endorsed by the business community, then the United States would be doomed once more to that morass of confusion and failure into which business rule has invariably plunged us through our history.

There is no easy answer to this conflict of principles between civil liberty and national security. The practical results thus must depend too much for comfort upon the restraint and wisdom of individuals. This responsibility becomes only one aspect of the great moral challenge which confronts us. If we cannot handle this conflict of principle soberly and responsibly, if we cannot rise to the world crisis, then we lack the qualities of greatness as a nation, and we can expect to pay the price of hysteria or of paralysis.

Justice Oliver Wendell Holmes:

THE STANDARD OF THE
"CLEAR AND PRESENT DANGER"

ON a single indictment, containing four counts, the five plaintiffs in error, hereinafter designated the defendants, were convicted of conspiring to violate provisions of the Espionage Act of Congress (p 3, Title I, of Act approved June 15, 1917, as amended May 16, 1918, 40 Stat. 443).

Each of the first three counts charged the defendants with conspiring, when the United States was at war with the Imperial Government of Germany, to unlawfully utter, print, write and publish: In the first count, "disloyal, scurrilous and abusive language about the form of Government of the United States"; in the second count, language "intended to bring the form of Government of the United States into contempt, scorn, contumely and disrepute"; and in the third count, language "intended to incite, provoke and encourage resistance to the United States in said war." The charge in the fourth count was that the defendants conspired "when the United States was at war with the Imperial German Government, ... unlawfully and wilfully, by utterance, writing, printing and publication, to urge, incite and advocate curtailment of production of things and products, to wit, ordnance and ammunition, necessary and essential to the prosecution of the war." The offenses were charged in the language of the act of Congress.

It was charged in each count of the indictment that it was a part of the conspiracy that the defendants would attempt to accomplish their unlawful purpose by printing, writing and distributing in the City of New York many copies of a leaflet or circular, printed in the English language, and of another printed in the Yiddish language, copies of which, properly identified, were attached to the indictment.

All of the five defendants were born in Russia. They were intelligent, had considerable schooling, and at the time they were arrested they had lived in the United States terms varying from five to ten years, but none of them had applied

The dissenting opinion in *Abrams et al v. United States*, 250 U. S. 616. The description of the facts in this case is taken from the majority opinion of the Court, written by Mr. Justice Clarke, which upheld the conviction of the five defendants.

for naturalization. Four of them testified as witnesses in their own behalf and of these, three frankly avowed that they were "rebels," "revolutionists," "anarchists," that they did not believe in government in any form, and they declared that they had no interest whatever in the Government of the United States. The fourth defendant testified that he was a "socialist" and believed in "a proper kind of government, not capitalistic," but in his classification the Government of the United States was "capitalistic."

It was admitted on the trial that the defendants had united to print and distribute the described circulars and that five thousand of them had been printed and distributed about the 22d day of August, 1918. The group had a meeting place in New York City, in rooms rented by defendant Abrams, under an assumed name, and there the subject of printing the circulars was discussed about two weeks before the defendants were arrested. The defendant Abrams, although not a printer, on July 27, 1918, purchased the printing outfit with which the circulars were printed and installed it in a basement room where the work was done at night. The circulars were distributed, some by throwing them from a window of a building where one of the defendants was employed and others secretly, in New York City.

Dissenting opinion of MR. JUSTICE HOLMES

This indictment is founded wholly upon the publication of two leaflets which I shall describe in a moment. The first count charges a conspiracy pending the war with Germany to publish abusive language about the form of government of the United States, laying the preparation and publishing of the first leaflet as overt acts. The second count charges a conspiracy pending the war to publish language intended to bring the form of government into contempt, laying the preparation and publishing of the two leaflets as overt acts. The third count alleges a conspiracy to encourage resistance to the United States in the same war and to attempt to effectuate the purpose by publishing the same leaflets. The fourth count lays a conspiracy to incite curtailment of production of things necessary to the prosecution of the war and to attempt to accomplish it by publishing the second leaflet to which I have referred.

The first of these leaflets says that the President's cowardly silence about the intervention in Russia reveals the hypocrisy of the plutocratic gang in Washington. It intimates that "German militarism combined with allied capitalism to crush the Russian revolution"— goes on that the tyrants of the world fight each other until they see a common enemy — working class enlightenment, when they combine to crush it; and that now militarism and capitalism combined, though not openly, to crush the Russian revolution. It says that there is only one enemy of the workers of the world and that is capitalism; that it is a crime for workers of America, &c., to fight the workers' republic of Russia, and ends "Awake! Awake, you Workers of the World! Revolutionists." A note adds "It is absurd to call us pro-German. We hate and despise German militarism more than do you hypocritical tyrants. We have more reasons for denouncing German militarism than has the coward of the White House."

The other leaflet, headed "Workers — Wake Up," with abusive language says that America together with the Allies will march for Russia to help the Czecko-Slovaks in their struggle against the Bolsheviki, and that this time the hypocrites shall not fool the Russian emigrants and friends of Russia in America. It tells the Russian emigrants that they now must spit in the face of the false military propaganda by which their sympathy and help to the prosecution of the war have been called forth and says that with the money they have lent or are going to lend "they will make bullets not only for the Germans but also for the Workers Soviets of Russia," and further, "Workers in the ammunition factories, you are producing bullets, bayonets, cannon, to murder not only the Germans, but also your dearest, best, who are in Russia and are fighting for freedom." It then appeals to the same Russian emigrants at some length not to consent to the "inquisitionary expedition to Russia," and says that the destruction of the Russian revolution is "the politics of the march to Russia." The leaflet winds up by saying "Workers, our reply to this barbaric intervention has to be a general strike!" and after a few words on the spirit of revolution, exhortations not to be afraid, and some usual tall talk ends "Woe unto those who will be in the way of progress. Let solidarity live! The Rebels."

· No argument seems to me necessary to show that these pronunciamentos in no way attack the form of government of the United States, or that they do not support either of the first two counts. What little I have to say about the third count may be postponed until I have considered the fourth. With regard to that it seems too plain to be denied that the suggestion to workers in the ammunition factories that they are producing bullets to murder their dearest, and the further advocacy of a general strike, both in the

second leaflet, do urge curtailment of production of things necessary to the prosecution of the war within the meaning of the Act of May 16, 1918, c. 75, 40 Stat. 443, amending p 3 of the earlier Act of 1917. But to make the conduct criminal that statute requires that it should be "with intent by such curtailment to cripple or hinder the United States in the prosecution of the war." It seems to me that no such intent is proved.

I am aware of course that the word intent as vaguely used in ordinary legal discussion means no more than knowledge at the time of the act that the consequences said to be intended will ensue. Even less than that will satisfy the general principle of civil and criminal liability. A man may have to pay damages, may be sent to prison, at common law might be hanged, if at the time of his act he knew facts from which common experience showed that the consequences would follow, whether he individually could foresee them or not. But, when words are used exactly, a deed is not done with intent to produce a consequence unless that consequence is the aim of the deed. It may be obvious, and obvious to the actor, that the consequence will follow, and he may be liable for it even if he regrets it, but he does not do the act with intent to produce it unless the aim to produce it is the proximate motive of the specific act, although there may be some deeper motive behind.

It seems to me that this statute must be taken to use its words in a strict and accurate sense. They would be absurd in any other. A patriot might think that we were wasting money on aeroplanes, or making more cannon of a certain kind than we needed, and might advocate curtailment with success, yet even if it turned out that the curtailment hindered and was thought by other minds to have been obviously likely to hinder the United States in the prosecution of the war, no one would hold such conduct a crime. I admit that my illustration does not answer all that might be said but it is enough to show what I think and to let me pass to a more important aspect of the case. I refer to the First Amendment to the Constitution that Congress shall make no law abridging the freedom of speech.

I never have seen any reason to doubt that the questions of law that alone were before this Court in the cases of *Schenck, Frohwerk* and *Debs*, 249 U. S. 47, 204, 211, were rightly decided. I do not doubt for a moment that by the same reasoning that would justify punishing persuasion to murder, the United States constitutionally may punish speech that produces or is intended to produce a clear and imminent danger that it will bring about forthwith certain substantive evils that the United States constitutionally may seek to prevent. The power undoubtedly is greater in time of war than in time of peace because war opens dangers that do not exist at other times.

But as against dangers peculiar to war, as against others, the principle of the right to free speech is always the same. It is only the present danger of immediate evil or an intent to bring it about that warrants Congress in setting a limit to the expression of opinion where private rights are not concerned. Congress certainly cannot forbid all effort to change the mind of the country. Now nobody can suppose that the surreptitious publishing of a silly leaflet by an unknown man, without more, would present any immediate danger that its opinions would hinder the success of the government arms or have any appreciable tendency to do so. Publishing those opinions for the very purpose of obstruct-

ing however, might indicate a greater danger and at any rate would have the quality of an attempt. So I assume that the second leaflet if published for the purposes alleged in the fourth count might be punishable. But it seems pretty clear to me that nothing less than that would bring these papers within the scope of this law. An actual intent in the sense that I have explained is necessary to constitute an attempt, where a further act of the same individual is required to complete the substantive crime, for reasons given in *Swift & Co.* v. *United States*, 196 U. S. 375, 396. It is necessary where the success of the attempt depends upon others because if that intent is not present the actor's aim may be accomplished without bringing about the evils sought to be checked. An intent to prevent interference with the revolution in Russia might have been satisfied without any hindrance to carrying on the war in which we were engaged.

I do not see how anyone can find the intent required by the statute in any of the defendants' words. The second leaflet is the only one that affords even a foundation for the charge, and there, without invoking the hatred of German militarism expressed in the former one, it is evident from the beginning to the end that the only object of the paper is to help Russia and stop American intervention there against the popular government — not to impede the United States in the war that it was carrying on. To say that two phrases taken literally might import a suggestion of conduct that would have interference with the war as an indirect and probably undesired effect seems to me by no means enough to show an attempt to produce that effect.

I return for a moment to the third count. That charges an intent to provoke resistance to the United States in its war with Germany. Taking the clause in the statute that deals with that in connection with the other elaborate provisions of the act, I think that resistance to the United States means some forcible act of opposition to some proceeding of the United States in pursuance of the war. I think the intent must be the specific intent that I have described and for the reasons that I have given I think that no such intent was proved or existed in fact. I also think that there is no hint at resistance to the United States as I construe the phrase.

In this case sentences of twenty years imprisonment have been imposed for the publishing of two leaflets that I believe the defendants had as much right to publish as the Government has to publish the Constitution of the United States now vainly invoked by them. Even if I am technically wrong and enough can be squeezed from these poor and puny anonymities to turn the color of legal litmus paper; I will add, even if what I think the necessary intent were shown; the most nominal punishment seems to me all that possibly could be inflicted, unless the defendants are to be made to suffer not for what the indictment alleges but for the creed that they avow — a creed that I believe to be the creed of ignorance and immaturity when honestly held, as I see no reason to doubt that it was held here, but which, although made the subject of examination at the trial, no one has a right even to consider in dealing with the charges before the Court.

Persecution for the expression of opinions seems to me perfectly logical. If you have no doubt of your premises or your power and want a certain result with all your heart you naturally express your wishes in law and sweep away all opposition. To allow opposition by speech seems to indicate that you think the

speech impotent, as when a man says that he has squared the circle, or that you do not care whole-heartedly for the result, or that you doubt either your power or your premises. But when men have realized that time has upset many fighting faiths, they may come to believe even more than they believe the very foundations of their own conduct that the ultimate good desired is better reached by free trade in ideas — that the best test of truth is the power of the thought to get itself accepted in the competition of the market, and that truth is the only ground upon which their wishes safely can be carried out. That at any rate is the theory of our Constitution. It is an experiment, as all life is an experiment. Every year if not every day we have to wager our salvation upon some prophecy based upon imperfect knowledge. While that experiment is part of our system I think that we should be eternally vigilant against attempts to check the expression of opinions that we loathe and believe to be fraught with death, unless they so imminently threaten immediate interference with the lawful and pressing purposes of the law that an immediate check is required to save the country. I wholly disagree with the argument of the Government that the First Amendment left the common law as to seditious libel in force. History seems to me against the notion. I had conceived that the United States through many years had shown its repentance for the Sedition Act of 1798, by repaying fines that it imposed. Only the emergency that makes it immediately dangerous to leave the correction of evil counsels to time warrants making any exception to the sweeping command, "Congress shall make no law . . . abridging the freedom of speech." Of course I am speaking only of expressions of opinion and exhortations, which were all that were uttered here, but I regret that I cannot put into more impressive words my belief that in their conviction upon this indictment the defendants were deprived of their rights under the Constitution of the United States.

Justice Felix Frankfurter:

POLITICAL LOYALTY IS PARAMOUNT OVER RELIGIOUS LOYALTY

A GRAVE responsibility confronts this Court whenever in course of litigation it must reconcile the conflicting claims of liberty and authority. But when the liberty invoked is liberty of conscience, and the authority is authority to safeguard the nation's fellowship, judicial conscience is put to its severest test. Of such a nature is the present controversy.

Lillian Gobitis, aged twelve, and her brother William, aged ten, were expelled from the public schools of Minersville, Pennsylvania, for refusing to salute the national flag as part of a daily school exercise. The local Board of Education required both teachers and pupils to participate in this ceremony. The ceremony is a familiar one. The right hand is placed on the breast and the following pledge recited in unison: "I pledge allegiance to my flag, and to the Republic for which it stands; one nation indivisible, with liberty and justice for all." While the words are spoken, teachers and pupils extend their right hands in salute to the flag. The Gobitis family are affiliated with "Jehovah's Witnesses," for whom the Bible as the Word of God is the supreme authority. The children had been brought up conscientiously to believe that such a gesture of respect for the flag was forbidden by command of Scripture.[1]

The Gobitis children were of an age for which Pennsylvania makes school attendance compulsory. Thus they were denied a free education, and their parents had to put them into private schools. To be relieved of the financial burden thereby entailed, their father, on behalf of the children and in his own behalf, brought this suit. He sought to enjoin the authorities from continuing to exact participation in the flag-salute ceremony as a condition of his children's attendance at the Minersville school. After trial of the issues, Judge Maris gave relief in the District Court, 24 F. Supp. 271, on the basis of a thoughtful opinion at a preliminary stage of the litigation, 21 F. Supp. 581; his decree was affirmed by the Circuit Court of Appeals, 108 F. 2d 683. Since this decision ran counter to several

[1] Reliance is especially placed on the following verses from Chapter 20 of Exodus:

"3. Thou shalt have no other gods before me.

"4. Thou shalt not make unto thee any graven image, or any likeness of any thing that is in heaven above, or that is in the earth beneath, or that is in the water under the earth:

"5. Thou shalt not bow down thyself to them, nor serve them: . . ."

Opinion of the Court in *Minersville School District v. Gobitis*, 310 U. S. 586, June 3, 1940.

per curiam dispositions of this Court, we granted *certiorari* to give the matter full reconsideration. 309 U. S. 645. By their able submissions, the Committee on the Bill of Rights of the American Bar Association and the American Civil Liberties Union, as friends of the Court, have helped us to our conclusion.

We must decide whether the requirement of participation in such a ceremony, exacted from a child who refuses upon sincere religious grounds, infringes without due process of law the liberty guaranteed by the Fourteenth Amendment.

Centuries of strife over the erection of particular dogmas as exclusive or all-comprehending faiths led to the inclusion of a guarantee for religious freedom in the Bill of Rights. The First Amendment, and the Fourteenth through its absorption of the First, sought to guard against repetition of those bitter religious struggles by prohibiting the establishment of a state religion and by securing to every sect the free exercise of its faith. So pervasive is the acceptance of this precious right that its scope is brought into question, as here, only when the conscience of individuals collides with the felt necessities of society.

Certainly the affirmative pursuit of one's convictions about the ultimate mystery of the universe and man's relation to it is placed beyond the reach of law. Government may not interfere with organized or individual expression of belief or disbelief. Propagation of belief — or even of disbelief — in the supernatural is protected, whether in church or chapel, mosque or synagogue, tabernacle or meeting-house. Likewise the Constitution assures generous immunity to the individual from imposition of penalties for offending, in the course of his own religious activities, the religious views of others, be they a minority or those who are dominant in government. *Cantwell v. Connecticut, ante,* p. 296.

But the manifold character of man's relations may bring his conception of religious duty into conflict with the secular interests of his fellow-men. When does the constitutional guarantee compel exemption from doing what society thinks necessary for the promotion of some great common end, or from a penalty for conduct which appears dangerous to the general good? To state the problem is to recall the truth that no single principle can answer all of life's complexities. The right to freedom of religious belief, however dissident and however obnoxious to the cherished beliefs of others — even of a majority — is itself the denial of an absolute. But to affirm that the freedom to follow conscience has itself no limits in the life of a society would deny that very plurality of principles which, as a matter of history, underlies protection of religious toleration. Compare Mr. Justice Holmes in *Hudson Water Co.* v. *Mc-Carter,* 209 U. S. 349, 355. Our present task, then, as so often the case with courts, is to reconcile two rights in order to prevent either from destroying the other. But, because in safeguarding conscience we are dealing with interests so subtle and so dear, every possible leeway should be given to the claims of religious faith.

In the judicial enforcement of religious freedom we are concerned with a historic concept. See Mr. Justice Cardozo in *Hamilton* v. *Regents,* 293 U. S. at 265. The religious liberty which the Constitution protects has never excluded legislation of general scope not directed against doctrinal loyalties of particular sects. Judicial nullification of legislation cannot be justified by attributing to the framers of the Bill of Rights views for which there is no historic warrant. Conscientious scruples have not, in the course of the long struggle for religious toleration, relieved the individual from obedience to a general law not aimed at the promotion or restriction of religious beliefs. The mere possession of religious convictions which contradict the relevant concerns of a political society does not relieve the citizen from the discharge of political responsibilities. The necessity for this adjustment has again and again been recognized. In a number of situations the exertion of political authority has been sustained, while basic considerations of religious freedom have been left inviolate. *Reynolds* v. *United States*, 98 U. S. 145; *Davis* v. *Beason*, 133 U. S. 333; *Selective Draft Law Cases*, 245 U. S. 366; *Hamilton* v. *Regents*, 293 U. S. 265. In all these cases the general laws in question, upheld in their application to those who refused obedience from religious conviction, were manifestations of specific powers of government deemed by the legislature essential to secure and maintain that orderly, tranquil, and free society without which religious toleration itself is unattainable. Nor does the freedom of speech assured by Due Process move in a more absolute circle of immunity than that enjoyed by religious freedom. Even if it were assumed that freedom of speech goes beyond the historic concept of full opportunity to utter and to disseminate views, however heretical or offensive to dominant opinion, and includes freedom from conveying what may be deemed an implied but rejected affirmation, the question remains whether school children, like the Gobitis children, must be excused from conduct required of all the other children in the promotion of national cohesion. We are dealing with an interest inferior to none in the hierarchy of legal values. National unity is the basis of national security. To deny the

legislature the right to select appropriate means for its attainment presents a totally different order of problem from that of the propriety of subordinating the possible ugliness of littered streets to the free expression of opinion through distribution of handbills. Compare *Schneider* v. *State*, 308 U. S. 147.

Situations like the present are phases of the profoundest problem confronting a democracy — the problem which Lincoln cast in memorable dilemma: "Must a government of necessity be too *strong* for the liberties of its people, or too *weak* to maintain its own existence?" No mere textual reading or logical talisman can solve the dilemma. And when the issue demands judicial determination, it is not the personal notion of judges of what wise adjustment requires which must prevail.

Unlike the circumstances we have cited, the case before us is not concerned with an exertion of legislative power for the promotion of some specific need or interest of secular society — the protection of the family, the promotion of health, the common defense, the raising of public revenues to defray the cost of government. But all these specific activities of government presuppose the existence of an organized political society. The ultimate foundation of a free society is the binding tie of cohesive sentiment. Such a sentiment is fostered by all those agencies of the mind and spirit which may serve to gather up the traditions of a people, transmit them from generation to generation, and thereby create that continuity of a treasured common life which constitutes a civilization. "We live by symbols." The flag is the symbol of our national unity, transcending all internal differences, however large, within the framework of the Constitution. This Court has had occasion to say that

". . . the flag is the symbol of the Nation's power, the emblem of freedom in its truest, best sense . . . it signifies government resting on the consent of the governed; liberty regulated by law; the protection of the weak against the strong; security against the exercise of arbitrary power; and absolute safety for free institutions against foreign aggression." *Halter* v. *Nebraska*, 205 U. S. 34, 43. And see *United States* v. *Gettysburg Electric Ry. Co.*, 160 U. S. 668.

The case before us must be viewed as though the legislature of Pennsylvania had itself formally directed the flag-salute for the children of Minersville; had made no exemption for children whose parents were possessed of conscientious scruples like those of the Gobitis family; and had indicated its belief in the desirable ends to be secured by having its public school children share a common experience at those periods of development when their minds are supposedly receptive to its assimilation, by an exercise appropriate in time and place and setting, and one designed to evoke in them appreciation of the nation's hopes and dreams, its sufferings and sacrifices. The precise issue, then, for us to decide is whether the legislatures of the various states and the authorities in a thousand counties and school districts of this country are barred from determining the appropriateness of various means to evoke that unifying sentiment without which there can ultimately be no liberties, civil or religious. To stigmatize legislative judgment in providing for this universal gesture of respect for the symbol of our national life in the setting of the common school as a lawless inroad on that freedom of conscience which the Constitution protects, would amount to no less than the pronouncement of pedagogical and psychological dogma in a field where courts possess no marked and certainly

no controlling competence. The influences which help toward a common feeling for the common country are manifold. Some may seem harsh and others no doubt are foolish. Surely, however, the end is legitimate. And the effective means for its attainment are still so uncertain and so unauthenticated by science as to preclude us from putting the widely prevalent belief in flag-saluting beyond the pale of legislative power. It mocks reason and denies our whole history to find in the allowance of a requirement to salute our flag on fitting occasions the seeds of sanction for obeisance to a leader.

The wisdom of training children in patriotic impulses by those compulsions which necessarily pervade so much of the educational process is not for our independent judgment. Even were we convinced of the folly of such a measure, such belief would be no proof of its unconstitutionality. For ourselves, we might be tempted to say that the deepest patriotism is best engendered by giving unfettered scope to the most crotchety beliefs. Perhaps it is best, even from the standpoint of those interests which ordinances like the one under review seek to promote, to give to the least popular sect leave from conformities like those here in issue. But the courtroom is not the arena for debating issues of educational policy. It is not our province to choose among competing considerations in the subtle process of securing effective loyalty to the traditional ideals of democracy, while respecting at the same time individual idiosyncrasies among a people so diversified in racial origins and religious allegiances. So to hold would in effect make us the school board for the country. That authority has not been given to this Court, nor should we assume it.

We are dealing here with the formative period in the development of citizenship. Great diversity of psychological and ethical opinion exists among us concerning the best way to train children for their place in society. Because of these differences and because of reluctance to permit a single, ironcast system of education to be imposed upon a nation compounded of so many strains, we have held that, even though public education is one of our most cherished democratic institutions, the Bill of Rights bars a state from compelling all children to attend the public schools. *Pierce* v. *Society of Sisters*, 268 U. S. 510. But it is a very different thing for this Court to exercise censorship over the conviction of legislatures that a particular program or exercise will best promote in the minds of children who attend the common schools an attachment to the institutions of their country.

What the school authorities are really asserting is the right to awaken in the child's mind considerations as to the significance of the flag contrary to those implanted by the parent. In such an attempt the state is normally at a disadvantage in competing with the parent's authority, so long — and this is the vital aspect of religious toleration — as parents are unmolested in their right to counteract by their own persuasiveness the wisdom and rightness of those loyalties which the state's educational system is seeking to promote. Except where the transgression of constitutional liberty is too plain for argument, personal freedom is best maintained — so long as the remedial channels of the democratic process remain open and unobstructed — when it is ingrained in a people's habits and not enforced against popular policy by the coercion of adjudicated law. That the flag-salute is an allowable portion of a school program for those who do not invoke conscientious scruples is surely not debatable. But for us to insist that, though the ceremony may be required, exceptional immunity must be given to dissidents, is to maintain that there is no basis for a legislative judgment that such an exemption might introduce elements of difficulty into the school discipline, might cast doubts in the minds of the other children which would themselves weaken the effect of the exercise.

The preciousness of the family relation, the authority and independence which give dignity to parenthood, indeed the enjoyment of all freedom, presuppose the kind of ordered society which is summarized by our flag. A society which is dedicated to the preservation of these ultimate values of civilization may in self-protection utilize the educational process for inculcating those almost unconscious feelings which bind men together in a comprehending loyalty, whatever may be their lesser differences and difficulties. That is to say, the process may be utilized so long as men's right to believe as they please, to win others to their way of belief, and their right to assemble in their chosen places of worship for the devotional ceremonies of their faith, are all fully respected.

Judicial review, itself a limitation on popular government, is a fundamental part of our constitutional scheme. But to the legislature no less than to courts is committed the guardianship of deeply-cherished liberties. See *Missouri, K. & T. Ry. Co.* v. *May*, 194 U. S. 267, 270. Where all the effective means of inducing political changes are left free from interference, education in the abandonment of foolish legislation is itself a training in liberty. To fight out the wise use of legislative authority in the forum of public opinion and before legislative assemblies rather than to transfer such a contest to the judicial arena, serves to vindicate the self-confidence of a free people.

Justice Robert H. Jackson:

POLITICAL LOYALTY IS NOT PARAMOUNT OVER RELIGIOUS LOYALTY

FOLLOWING the decision by this Court on June 3, 1940, in *Minersville School District v. Gobitis,* 310 U. S. 586, the West Virginia legislature amended its statutes to require all schools therein to conduct courses of instruction in history, civics, and in the Constitutions of the United States and of the State "for the purpose of teaching, fostering and perpetuating the ideals, principles and spirit of Americanism, and increasing the knowledge of the organization and machinery of the government." Appellant Board of Education was directed, with advice of the State Superintendent of Schools, to "prescribe the courses of study covering these subjects" for public schools. The Act made it the duty of private, parochial and denominational schools to prescribe courses of study "similar to those required for the public schools."

The Board of Education on January 9, 1942, adopted a resolution containing recitals taken largely from the Court's *Gobitis* opinion and ordering that the salute to the flag become "a regular part of the program of activities in the public schools," that all teachers and pupils "shall be required to participate in the salute honoring the Nation represented by the Flag; provided, however, that refusal to salute the Flag be regarded as an act of insubordination, and shall be dealt with accordingly."

The resolution originally required the "commonly accepted salute to the Flag" which it defined. Objections to the salute as "being too much like Hitler's" were raised by the Parent and Teachers Association, the Boy and Girl Scouts, the Red Cross, and the Federation of Women's Clubs. Some modification appears to have been made in deference to these objections, but no concession was made to Jehovah's Witnesses. What is now required is the "stiff-arm" salute, the saluter to keep the right hand raised with palm turned up while the following is repeated: "I pledge allegiance to the Flag of the United States of America and to the Republic for which it stands; one Nation, indivisible, with liberty and justice for all."

Failure to conform is "insubordination" dealt with by expulsion. Readmission is denied by statute until compliance. Meanwhile the expelled child is "unlawfully absent" and may be proceeded against as a delinquent. His parents or guardians are liable to prosecution, and if convicted are subject to fine not exceeding $50 and jail term not exceeding thirty days.

Appellees, citizens of the United States and of West Virginia, brought suit in the United States District Court for themselves and others similarly situated asking its injunction to restrain enforcement of these laws and regulations against

Opinion of the Court in *West Virginia State Board of Education et al v. Barnette et al,* 319 U. S. 624, June 14, 1943.

Jehovah's Witnesses. The Witnesses are an unincorporated body teaching that the obligation imposed by law of God is superior to that of laws enacted by temporal government. Their religious beliefs include a literal version of Exodus, Chapter 20, verses 4 and 5, which says: "Thou shalt not make unto thee any graven image, or any likeness of anything that is in heaven above, or that is in the earth beneath, or that is in the water under the earth; thou shalt not bow down thyself to them nor serve them." They consider that the flag is an "image" within this command. For this reason they refuse to salute it.

Children of this faith have been expelled from school and are threatened with exclusion for no other cause. Officials threaten to send them to reformatories maintained for criminally inclined juveniles. Parents of such children have been prosecuted and are threatened with prosecutions for causing delinquency.

The Board of Education moved to dismiss the complaint setting forth these facts and alleging that the law and regulations are an unconstitutional denial of religious freedom, and of freedom of speech, and are invalid under the "due process" and "equal protection" clauses of the Fourteenth Amendment to the Federal Constitution. The cause was submitted on the pleadings to a District Court of three judges. It restrained enforcement as to the plaintiffs and those of that class. The Board of Education brought the case here by direct appeal.

This case calls upon us to reconsider a precedent decision, as the Court throughout its history often has been required to do. Before turning to the *Gobitis* case, however, it is desirable to notice certain characteristics by which this controversy is distinguished.

The freedom asserted by these appel-lees does not bring them into collision with rights asserted by any other individual. It is such conflicts which most frequently require intervention of the State to determine where the rights of one end and those of another begin. But the refusal of these persons to participate in the ceremony does not interfere with or deny rights of others to do so. Nor is there any question in this case that their behavior is peaceable and orderly. The sole conflict is between authority and rights of the individual. The State asserts power to condition access to public education on making a prescribed sign and profession and at the same time to coerce attendance by punishing both parent and child. The latter stand on a right of self-determination in matters that touch individual opinion and personal attitude.

As the present CHIEF JUSTICE said in dissent in the *Gobitis* case, the State may "require teaching by instruction and study of all in our history and in the structure and organization of our government, including the guaranties of civil liberty, which tend to inspire patriotism and love of country." 310 U. S. at 604. Here, however, we are dealing with a compulsion of students to declare a belief. They are not merely made acquainted with the flag salute so that they may be informed as to what it is or even what it means. The issue here is whether this slow and easily neglected route to aroused loyalties constitutionally may be short-cut by substituting a compulsory salute and slogan. This issue is not prejudiced by the Court's previous holding that where a State, without compelling attendance, extends college facilities to pupils who voluntarily enroll, it may prescribe military training as part of the course without offense to the Constitution. It was held that those who take advantage of its opportunities may not on ground of conscience refuse compliance with such conditions. *Hamilton* v. *Regents*, 293 U. S. 245. In the present case attendance is not optional. That case is also to be distinguished from the present one, because, independently of college privileges or requirements, the State has power to raise militia and impose the duties of service therein upon its citizens.

There is no doubt that, in connection with the pledges, the flag salute is a form of utterance. Symbolism is a primitive but effective way of communicating ideas. The use of an emblem or flag to symbolize some system, idea, institution, or personality, is a short cut from mind to mind. Causes and nations, political parties, lodges and ecclesiastical groups seek to knit the loyalty of their followings to a flag or banner, a color or design. The State announces rank, function, and authority through crowns and maces, uniforms and black robes; the church speaks through the Cross, the Crucifix, the altar and shrine, and clerical raiment. Symbols of State often convey political ideas just as religious symbols come to convey theological ones. Associated with many of these symbols are appropriate gestures of acceptance or respect: a salute, a bowed or bared head, a bended knee. A person gets from a symbol the meaning he puts into it, and what is one man's comfort and inspiration is another's jest and scorn.

Over a decade ago Chief Justice Hughes led this Court in holding that the display of a red flag as a symbol of opposition by peaceful and legal means to organized government was protected by the free speech guaranties of the Constitution. *Stromberg* v. *California*, 283 U. S. 359. Here it is the State that employs a flag as a symbol of adherence to government as presently organized. It requires the individual to communicate by word and sign his acceptance of the political ideas it thus bespeaks. Objection to this form of communication when coerced is an old one, well known to the framers of the Bill of Rights.

It is also to be noted that the compulsory flag salute and pledge requires affirmation of a belief and an attitude of mind. It is not clear whether the regulation contemplates that pupils forego any contrary convictions of their own and become unwilling converts to the prescribed ceremony or whether it will be acceptable if they simulate assent by words without belief and by a gesture barren of meaning. It is now a commonplace that censorship or suppression of expression of opinion is tolerated by our Constitution only when the expression presents a clear and present danger of action of a kind the State is empowered to prevent and punish. It would seem that involuntary affirmation could be commanded only on even more immediate and urgent grounds than silence. But here the power of compulsion is invoked without any allegation that remaining passive during a flag salute ritual creates a clear and present danger that would justify an effort even to muffle expression. To sustain the compulsory flag salute we are required to say that a Bill of Rights which guards the individual's right to speak his own mind, left it open to public authorities to compel him to utter what is not in his mind.

Whether the First Amendment to the Constitution will permit officials to order observance of ritual of this nature does not depend upon whether as a voluntary exercise we would think it to be good, bad or merely innocuous. Any credo of nationalism is likely to include what some disapprove or to omit what others think essential, and to give off different over-tones as it takes on different accents or interpretations. If official power exists to coerce acceptance of any patriotic creed, what it shall contain cannot be decided by courts, but must be largely discretionary with the ordaining authority, whose power to prescribe would no doubt include power to amend. Hence validity of the asserted power to force an American citizen publicly to profess any statement of belief or to engage in any ceremony of assent to one, presents questions of power that must be considered independently of any idea we may have as to the utility of the ceremony in question.

Nor does the issue as we see it turn on one's possession of particular religious views or the sincerity with which they are held. While religion supplies appellees' motive for enduring the discomforts of making the issue in this case, many citizens who do not share these religious views hold such a compulsory rite to infringe constitutional liberty of the individual. It is not necessary to inquire whether non-conformist beliefs will exempt from the duty to salute unless we first find power to make the salute a legal duty.

The *Gobitis* decision, however, *assumed,* as did the argument in that case and in this, that power exists in the State to impose the flag salute discipline upon school children in general. The court only examined and rejected a claim based on religious beliefs of immunity from an unquestioned general rule. The question which underlies the flag salute controversy is whether such a ceremony so touching matters of opinion and political attitude may be imposed upon the individual by official authority under powers committed to any political organization under our Constitution. We examine rather than assume existence of this power and, against this broader definition of issues in this case, reexamine specific grounds assigned for the *Gobitis* decision.

1. It was said that the flag-salute controversy confronted the Court with "the problem which Lincoln cast in memorable dilemma: 'Must a government of necessity be too *strong* for the liberties of its people, or too *weak* to maintain its own existence?'" and that the answer must be in favor of strength. *Minersville School District v. Gobitis, supra,* at 596.

We think these issues may be examined free of pressure or restraint growing out of such considerations.

It may be doubted whether Mr. Lincoln would have thought that the strength of government to maintain itself would be impressively vindicated by our confirming power of the State to expel a handful of children from school. Such oversimplification, so handy in political debate, often lacks the precision necessary to postulates of judicial reasoning. If validly applied to this problem, the utterance cited would resolve every issue of power in favor of those in authority and would require us to override every liberty thought to weaken or delay execution of their policies.

Government of limited power need not be anemic government. Assurance that rights are secure tends to diminish fear and jealousy of strong government, and by making us feel safe to live under it makes for its better support. Without promise of a limiting Bill of Rights it is doubtful if our Constitution could have mustered enough strength to enable its ratification. To enforce those rights today is not to choose weak government over strong government. It is only to adhere as a means of strength to individual freedom of mind in preference to officially disciplined uniformity for which history indicates a disappointing and disastrous end.

The subject now before us exemplifies this principle. Free public education, if faithful to the ideal of secular instruction and political neutrality, will not be partisan or enemy of any class, creed, party, or faction. If it is to impose any ideological discipline, however, each party or denomination must seek to control, or failing that, to weaken the influence of the educational system. Observance of the limitations of the Constitution will not weaken government in the field appropriate for its exercise.

2. It was also considered in the *Gobitis* case that functions of educational officers in States, counties and school districts were such that to interfere with their authority "would in effect make us the school board for the country." *Id.* at 598.

The Fourteenth Amendment, as now applied to the States, protects the citizen against the State itself and all of its creatures — Boards of Education not excepted. These have, of course, important, delicate, and highly discretionary functions, but none that they may not perform within the limits of the Bill of Rights. That they are educating the young for citizenship is reason for scrupulous protection of Constitutional freedoms of the individual, if we are not to strangle the free mind at its source and teach youth to discount important principles of our government as mere platitudes.

Such Boards are numerous and their territorial jurisdiction often small. But small and local authority may feel less sense of responsibility to the Constitution, and agencies of publicity may be less vigilant in calling it to account. The

action of Congress in making flag observance voluntary and respecting the conscience of the objector in a matter so vital as raising the Army contrasts sharply with these local regulations in matters relatively trivial to the welfare of the nation. There are village tyrants as well as village Hampdens, but none who acts under color of law is beyond reach of the Constitution.

3. The *Gobitis* opinion reasoned that this is a field "where courts possess no marked and certainly no controlling competence," that it is committed to the legislatures as well as the courts to guard cherished liberties and that it is constitutionally appropriate to "fight out the wise use of legislative authority in the forum of public opinion and before legislative assemblies rather than to transfer such a contest to the judicial arena," since all the "effective means of inducing political changes are left free." *Id.* at 597–598, 600.

The very purpose of a Bill of Rights was to withdraw certain subjects from the vicissitudes of political controversy, to place them beyond the reach of majorities and officials and to establish them as legal principles to be applied by the courts. One's right to life, liberty, and property, to free speech, a free press, freedom of worship and assembly, and other fundamental rights may not be submitted to vote; they depend on the outcome of no elections.

In weighing arguments of the parties it is important to distinguish between the due process clause of the Fourteenth Amendment as an instrument for transmitting the principles of the First Amendment and those cases in which it is applied for its own sake. The test of legislation which collides with the Fourteenth Amendment, because it also collides with the principles of the First, is much more definite than the test when only the Fourteenth is involved. Much of the vagueness of the due process clause disappears when the specific prohibitions of the First become its standard. The right of a State to regulate, for example, a public utility may well include, so far as the due process test is concerned, power to impose all of the restrictions which a legislature may have a "rational basis" for adopting. But freedoms of speech and of press, of assembly, and of worship may not be infringed on such slender grounds. They are susceptible of restriction only to prevent grave and immediate danger to interests which the State may lawfully protect. It is important to note that while it is the Fourteenth Amendment which bears directly upon the State it is the more specific limiting principles of the First Amendment that finally govern this case.

Nor does our duty to apply the Bill of Rights to assertions of official authority depend upon our possession of marked competence in the field where the invasion of rights occurs. True, the task of translating the majestic generalities of the Bill of Rights, conceived as part of the pattern of liberal government in the eighteenth century, into concrete restraints on officials dealing with the problems of the twentieth century, is one to disturb self-confidence. These principles grew in soil which also produced a philosophy that the individual was the center of society, that his liberty was attainable through mere absence of governmental restraints, and that government should be entrusted with few controls and only the mildest supervision over men's affairs. We must transplant these rights to a soil in which the *laissez-faire* concept or principle of non-interference has withered at least as to economic affairs, and social advancements are increasingly sought through closer integration of society and

through expanded and strengthened governmental controls. These changed conditions often deprive precedents of reliability and cast us more than we would choose upon our own judgment. But we act in these matters not by authority of our competence but by force of our commissions. We cannot, because of modest estimates of our competence in such specialties as public education, withhold the judgment that history authenticates as the function of this Court when liberty is infringed.

4. Lastly, and this is the very heart of the *Gobitis* opinion, it reasons that "National unity is the basis of national security," that the authorities have "the right to select appropriate means for its attainment," and hence reaches the conclusion that such compulsory measures toward "national unity" are constitutional. *Id.* at 595. Upon the verity of this assumption depends our answer in this case.

National unity as an end which officials may foster by persuasion and example is not in question. The problem is whether under our Constitution compulsion as here employed is a permissible means for its achievement.

Struggles to coerce uniformity of sentiment in support of some end thought essential to their time and country have been waged by many good as well as by evil men. Nationalism is a relatively recent phenomenon but at other times and places the ends have been racial or territorial security, support of a dynasty or regime, and particular plans for saving souls. As first and moderate methods to attain unity have failed, those bent on its accomplishment must resort to an ever-increasing severity. As governmental pressure toward unity becomes greater, so strife becomes more bitter as to whose unity it shall be. Probably no deeper division of our people could proceed from any provocation than from finding it necessary to choose what doctrine and whose program public educational officials shall compel youth to unite in embracing. Ultimate futility of such attempts to compel coherence is the lesson of every such effort from the Roman drive to stamp out Christianity as a disturber of its pagan unity, the Inquisition, as a means to religious and dynastic unity, the Siberian exiles as a means to Russian unity, down to the fast failing efforts of our present totalitarian enemies. Those who begin coercive elimination of dissent soon find themselves exterminating dissenters. Compulsory unification of opinion achieves only the unanimity of the graveyard.

It seems trite but necessary to say that the First Amendment to our Constitution was designed to avoid these ends by avoiding these beginnings. There is no mysticism in the American concept of the State or of the nature or origin of its authority. We set up government by consent of the governed, and the Bill of Rights denies those in power any legal opportunity to coerce that consent. Authority here is to be controlled by public opinion, not public opinion by authority.

The case is made difficult not because the principles of its decision are obscure but because the flag involved is our own. Nevertheless, we apply the limitations of the Constitution with no fear that freedom to be intellectually and spiritually diverse or even contrary will disintegrate the social organization. To believe that patriotism will not flourish if patriotic ceremonies are voluntary and spontane-

ous instead of a compulsory routine is to make an unflattering estimate of the appeal of our institutions to free minds. We can have intellectual individualism and the rich cultural diversities that we owe to exceptional minds only at the price of occasional eccentricity and abnormal attitudes. When they are so harmless to others or to the State as those we deal with here, the price is not too great. But freedom to differ is not limited to things that do not matter much. That would be a mere shadow of freedom. The test of its substance is the right to differ as to things that touch the heart of the existing order.

If there is any fixed star in our constitutional constellation, it is that no official, high or petty, can prescribe what shall be orthodox in politics, nationalism, religion, or other matters of opinion or force citizens to confess by word or act their faith therein. If there are any circumstances which permit an exception, they do not now occur to us.

We think the action of the local authorities in compelling the flag salute and pledge transcends constitutional limitations on their power and invades the sphere of intellect and spirit which it is the purpose of the First Amendment to our Constitution to reserve from all official control.

The decision of this Court in *Minersville School District v. Gobitis* and the holdings of those few *per curiam* decisions which preceded and foreshadowed it are overruled, and the judgment enjoining enforcement of the West Virginia Regulation is

Affirmed.

THE CASE OF THE ELEVEN COMMUNISTS

Editor's Note

The eleven Communist leaders were convicted under the Smith Act of 1940, relevant portions of which provide as follows:

Sec. 2: (a) It shall be unlawful for any person —

(1) to knowingly or wilfully advocate, abet, advise, or teach the duty, necessity, desirability, or propriety of overthrowing or destroying any government in the United States by force or violence, or by the assassination of any officer of such government.

(2) with intent to cause the overthrow or destruction of any government in the United States, to print, publish, edit, issue, circulate, sell, distribute, or publicly display any written or printed matter advocating, advising, or teaching the duty, necessity, desirability, or propriety of overthrowing or destroying any government in the United States by force or violence;

(3) to organize or help to organize any society, group, or assembly of persons who teach, advocate, or encourage the overthrow or destruction of any government in the United States by force or violence; or to be or become a member of, or affiliate with, any such society, group, or assembly of persons, knowing the purpose thereof.

Sec. 3: (b) It shall be unlawful for any person to commit, or to conspire to commit, any of the acts prohibited by the provisions of . . . this title.

The Government summary of the charges against the eleven men asserted that from April 1, 1945, until July, 1948, they "unlawfully, wilfully, and knowingly conspired with each other and with other persons unknown to the grand jury (1) to organize as the Communist Party of the United States of America a society, group and assembly of persons who teach and advocate the overthrow and destruction of the Government of the United States by force and violence, and (2) knowingly and wilfully to advocate and teach the duty and necessity of overthrowing and destroying the Government of the United States by force and violence. The indictment alleged that Section 2 of the Smith Act proscribes these acts and that the conspiracy to take such action is a violation of Section 3 of the act . . ."

SUPREME COURT OF THE UNITED STATES

No. 336. — OCTOBER TERM, 1950.

Eugene Dennis, John B. Williamson, Jacob Stachel, Robert G. Thompson, Benjamin J. Davis, Jr., Henry Winston, John Gates, Irving Potash, Gilbert Green, Carl Winter and Gus Hall, Petitioners, *v.* United States of America.	On Writ of Certiorari to the United States Court of Appeals for the Second Circuit.

[June 4, 1951.]

MR. JUSTICE JACKSON, *Concurring*

This prosecution is the latest of never-ending, because never successful, quests for some legal formula that will secure an existing order against revolutionary radicalism. It requires us to reappraise, in the light of our own times and conditions, constitutional doctrines devised under other circumstances to strike a balance between authority and liberty.

Activity here charged to be criminal is conspiracy — that defendants conspired to teach and advocate, and to organize the Communist Party to teach and advocate, overthrow and destruction of the Government by force and violence. There is no charge of actual violence or attempt at overthrow.

The principal reliance of the defense in this Court is that the conviction cannot stand under the Constitution because the conspiracy of these defendants presents no "clear and present danger" of imminent or foreseeable overthrow.

I.

The statute before us repeats a pattern, originally devised to combat the wave of anarchistic terrorism that plagued this country about the turn of the century, which lags at least two generations behind Communist Party techniques.

Anarchism taught a philosophy of extreme individualism and hostility to government and property. Its avowed aim was a more just order, to be achieved by violent destruction of all government. Anarchism's sporadic and uncoordinated acts of terror were not integrated with an effective revolutionary machine, but the Chicago Haymarket riots of 1886, attempted murder of the industrialist Frick, attacks on state officials, and assassination of President McKinley in 1901, were fruits of its preaching.

However, extreme individualism was not conducive to cohesive and disci-plined organization. Anarchism fell into disfavor among incendiary radicals, many of whom shifted their allegiance to the rising Communist Party. Meanwhile, in Europe anarchism had been displaced by Bolshevism as the doctrine and strategy of social and political upheaval. Led by intellectuals hardened by revolutionary experience, it was a more sophisticated, dynamic and realistic movement. Establishing a base in the Soviet Union, it founded an aggressive international Communist apparatus which has modeled and directed a revolutionary movement able only to harass our own country. But it has seized control of a dozen other countries.

Communism, the antithesis of anarchism, appears today as a closed system of thought representing Stalin's version of Lenin's version of Marxism. As an ideology, it is not one of spontaneous protest arising from American working-class experience. It is a complicated system of assumptions, based on European history and conditions, shrouded in an obscure and ambiguous vocabulary, which allures our ultrasophisticated intelligentsia more than our hard-headed working people. From time to time it champions all manner of causes and grievances and makes alliances that may add to its foothold in government or embarrass the authorities.

The Communist Party, nevertheless, does not seek its strength primarily in numbers. Its aim is a relatively small party whose strength is in selected, dedicated, indoctrinated, and rigidly disciplined members. From established policy it tolerates no deviation and no debate. It seeks members that are, or may be, secreted in strategic posts in transportation, communications, industry, government, and especially in labor unions where it can compel employers to accept and retain its members. It also seeks to infiltrate and control organizations of professional and other groups. Through these placements in positions of power it seeks a leverage over society that will make up in power of coercion what it lacks in power of persuasion.

The Communists have no scruples against sabotage, terrorism, assassination, or mob disorder; but violence is not with them, as with the anarchists, an end in itself. The Communist Party advocates force only when prudent and profitable. Their strategy of stealth precludes premature or uncoordinated outbursts of violence, except, of course, when the blame will be placed on shoulders other than their own. They resort to violence as to truth, not as a principle but as an expedient. Force or violence, as they would resort to it, may never be necessary, because infiltration and deception may be enough.

Force would be utilized by the Communist Party not to destroy government but for its capture. The Communist recognizes that an established government in control of modern technology cannot be overthrown by force until it is about ready to fall of its own weight. Concerted uprising, therefore, is to await that contingency and revolution is seen, not as a sudden episode, but as the consummation of a long process.

The United States, fortunately, has experienced Communism only in its preparatory stages and for its pattern of final action must look abroad. Russia, of course, was the pilot Communist revolution, which to the Marxist confirms the Party's assumptions and points its destiny. But Communist technique in the overturn of a free government was disclosed by the *coup d'état* in which they seized power in Czechoslovakia. There the Communist Party during its preparatory stage claimed and received protec-

tion for its freedoms of speech, press, and assembly. Pretending to be but another political party, it eventually was conceded participation in government, where it entrenched reliable members chiefly in control of police and information services. When the government faced a foreign and domestic crisis, the Communist Party had established a leverage strong enough to threaten civil war. In a period of confusion the Communist plan unfolded and the underground organization came to the surface throughout the country in the form chiefly of labor "action committees." Communist officers of the unions took over transportation and allowed only persons with party permits to travel. Communist printers took over the newspapers and radio and put out only party-approved versions of events. Possession was taken of telegraph and telephone systems and communications were cut off wherever directed by party heads. Communist unions took over the factories, and in the cities a partisan distribution of food was managed by the Communist organization. A virtually bloodless abdication by the elected government admitted the Communists to power, whereupon they instituted a reign of oppression and terror, and ruthlessly denied to all others the freedoms which had sheltered their conspiracy.

II.

The foregoing is enough to indicate that, either by accident or design, the Communist stratagem outwits the anti-anarchist pattern of statute aimed against "overthrow by force and violence" if qualified by the doctrine that only "clear and present danger" of accomplishing that result will sustain the prosecution.

The "clear and present danger" test was an innovation by Mr. Justice Holmes in the *Schenck* case, reiterated and refined by him and Mr. Justice Brandeis in later cases, all arising before the era of World War II revealed the subtlety and efficacy of modernized revolutionary techniques used by totalitarian parties. In those cases, they were faced with convictions under so-called criminal syndicalism statutes aimed at anarchists but which, loosely construed, had been applied to punish socialism, pacifism, and left-wing ideologies, the charges often resting on far-fetched inferences which, if true, would establish only technical or trivial violations. They proposed "clear and present danger" as a test for the sufficiency of evidence in particular cases.

I would save it, unmodified, for application as a "rule of reason" in the kind of case for which it was devised. When the issue is criminality of a hot-headed speech on a street corner, or circulation of a few incendiary pamphlets, or parading by some zealots behind a red flag, or refusal of a handful of school children to salute our flag, it is not beyond the capacity of the judicial process to gather, comprehend, and weigh the necessary materials for decision whether it is a clear and present danger of substantive evil or a harmless letting off of steam. It is not a prophecy, for the danger in such cases has matured by the time of trial or it was never present. The test applies and has meaning where a conviction is sought to be based on a speech or writing which does not directly or explicitly advocate a crime but to which such tendency is sought to be attributed by construction or by implication from external circumstances. The formula in such cases favors freedoms that are vital to our society, and, even if sometimes applied too generously, the consequences cannot be grave. But its recent expansion has extended, in particular to Communists, unprecedented immunities. Unless we are

to hold our Government captive in a judge-made verbal trap, we must approach the problem of a well-organized, nation-wide conspiracy, such as I have described, as realistically as our predecessors faced the trivialities that were being prosecuted until they were checked with a rule of reason.

I think reason is lacking for applying that test to this case.

If we must decide that this Act and its application are constitutional only if we are convinced that petitioner's conduct creates a "clear and present danger" of violent overthrow, we must appraise imponderables, including international and national phenomena which baffle the best informed foreign offices and our most experienced politicians. We would have to foresee and predict the effectiveness of Communist propaganda, opportunities for infiltration, whether, and when, a time will come that they consider propitious for action, and whether and how fast our existing government will deteriorate. And we would have to speculate as to whether an approaching Communist *coup* would not be anticipated by a nationalistic fascist movement. No doctrine can be sound whose application requires us to make a prophecy of that sort in the guise of a legal decision. The judicial process simply is not adequate to a trial of such far-flung issues. The answers given would reflect our own political predilections and nothing more.

The authors of the "clear and present danger" test never applied it to a case like this, nor would I. If applied as it is proposed here, it means that the Communist plotting is protected during its period of incubation; its preliminary stages of organization and preparation are immune from the law; the Government can move only after imminent action is manifest, when it would, of course, be too late.

III.

The highest degree of constitutional protection is due to the individual acting without conspiracy. But even an individual cannot claim that the Constitution protects him in advocating or teaching overthrow of government by force or violence. I should suppose no one would doubt that Congress has power to make such attempted overthrow a crime. But the contention is that one has the constitutional right to work up a public desire and will to do what it is a crime to attempt. I think direct incitement by speech or writing can be made a crime, and I think there can be a conviction without also proving that the odds favored its success by 99 to 1, or some other extremely high ratio. . . .

Of course, it is not always easy to distinguish teaching or advocacy in the sense of incitement from teaching or advocacy in the sense of exposition or explanation. It is a question of fact in each case.

IV.

What really is under review here is a conviction of conspiracy, after a trial for conspiracy, on an indictment charging conspiracy, brought under a statute outlawing conspiracy. With due respect to my colleagues, they seem to me to discuss anything under the sun except the law of conspiracy. One of the dissenting opinions even appears to chide me for "invoking the law of conspiracy." As that is the case before us, it may be more amazing that its reversal can be proposed without even considering the law of conspiracy.

The Constitution does not make conspiracy a civil right. The Court has never before done so and I think it should not do so now. Conspiracies of labor unions, trade associations, and news agencies have been condemned, although accomplished, evidenced and carried out, like the conspiracy here, chiefly by letter-writing, meetings, speeches and organization. Indeed, this Court seems, particularly in cases where the conspiracy has economic ends, to be applying its doctrines with increasing severity. While I consider criminal conspiracy a dragnet device capable of perversion into an instrument of injustice in the hands of a partisan or complacent judiciary, it has an established place in our system of law, and no reason appears for applying it only to concerted action claimed to disturb interstate commerce and withholding it from those claimed to undermine our whole Government.

The basic rationale of the law of conspiracy is that a conspiracy may be an evil in itself, independently of any other evil it seeks to accomplish. . . .

So far does this doctrine reach that it is well settled that Congress may make it a crime to conspire with others to do what an individual may lawfully do on his own. This principle is illustrated in conspiracies that violate the antitrust laws as sustained and applied by this Court. Although one may raise the prices of his own products, and many, acting without concert, may do so, the moment they conspire to that end they are punishable. The same principle is applied to organized labor. Any workman may quit his work for any reason, but concerted actions to the same end are in some circumstances forbidden. Labor Management Relations Act, 61 Stat. 136, § 8(b), 29 U. S. C. § 158(b). . . .

There is lamentation in the dissents about the injustice of conviction in the absence of some overt act. Of course, there has been no general uprising against the Government, but the record is replete with acts to carry out the conspiracy alleged, acts such as always are held sufficient to consummate the crime where the statute requires an overt act.

But the shorter answer is that no overt act is or need be required. . . .

Also, it is urged that since the conviction is for conspiracy to teach and advocate, and to organize the Communist Party to teach and advocate, the First Amendment is violated, because freedoms of speech and press protect teaching and advocacy regardless of what is taught or advocated. I have never thought that to be the law.

I do not suggest that Congress could punish conspiracy to advocate something, the doing of which it may not punish. Advocacy or exposition of the doctrine of communal property ownership, or any political philosophy unassociated with advocacy of its imposition by force or seizure of government by unlawful means could not be reached through conspiracy prosecution. But it is not forbidden to put down force or violence, it is not forbidden to punish its teaching or advocacy, and the end being punishable, there is no doubt of the power to punish conspiracy for the purpose.

The defense of freedom of speech or press has often been raised in conspiracy cases, because, whether committed by Communists, by businessmen, or by common criminals, it usually consists of words written or spoken, evidenced by letters, conversations, speeches or documents. Communication is the essence of every conspiracy, for only by it can common purpose and concert of action be brought about or be proved. However, when labor unions raised the defense of free speech against a conspiracy charge, we unanimously said:

It rarely has been suggested that the constitutional freedom for speech and press ex-

tends its immunity to speech or writing used as an integral part of conduct in violation of a valid criminal statute. We reject the contention now. . . .

Having held that a conspiracy alone is a crime and its consummation is another, it would be weird legal reasoning to hold that Congress could punish the one only if there was "clear and present danger" of the second. This would compel the Government to prove two crimes in order to convict for one.

When our constitutional provisions were written, the chief forces recognized as antagonists in the struggle between authority and liberty were the Government on the one hand and the individual citizen on the other. It was thought that if the state could be kept in its place the individual could take care of himself.

In more recent times these problems have been complicated by the intervention between the state and the citizen of permanently organized, well-financed, semisecret and highly disciplined political organizations. Totalitarian groups here and abroad perfected the technique of creating private paramilitary organizations to coerce both the public government and its citizens. These organizations assert as against our Government all of the constitutional rights and immunities of individuals and at the same time exercise over their followers much of the authority which they deny to the Government. The Communist Party realistically is a state within a state, an authoritarian dictatorship within a republic. It demands these freedoms, not for its members, but for the organized party. It denies to its own members at the same time the freedom to dissent, to debate, to deviate from the party line, and enforces its authoritarian rule by crude purges, if nothing more violent.

The law of conspiracy has been the chief means at the Government's disposal to deal with the growing problems created by such organizations. I happen to think it is an awkward and inept remedy, but I find no constitutional authority for taking this weapon from the Government. There is no constitutional right to "gang up" on the Government.

While I think there was power in Congress to enact this statute and that, as applied in this case, it cannot be held unconstitutional, I add that I have little faith in the long-range effectiveness of this conviction to stop the rise of the Communist movement. Communism will not go to jail with these Communists. No decision by this Court can forestall revolution whenever the existing government fails to command the respect and loyalty of the people and sufficient distress and discontent is allowed to grow up among the masses. Many failures by fallen governments attest that no government can long prevent revolution by outlawry. Corruption, ineptitude, inflation, oppressive taxation, militarization, injustice, and loss of leadership capable of intellectual initiative in domestic or foreign affairs are allies on which the Communists count to bring opportunity knocking to their door. Sometimes I think they may be mistaken. But the Communists are not building just for today — the rest of us might profit by their example.

MR. JUSTICE DOUGLAS, *Dissenting*

If this were a case where those who claimed protection under the First Amendment were teaching the techniques of sabotage, the assassination of the President, the filching of documents from public files, the planting of bombs, the art of street warfare, and the like, I would have no doubts. The freedom to speak is not absolute; the teaching of methods of terror and other seditious conduct should be beyond the pale along with obscenity and immorality. This case was argued as if those were the facts. The argument imported much seditious conduct into the record. That is easy and it has popular appeal, for the activities of Communists in plotting and scheming against the free world are common knowledge. But the fact is that no such evidence was introduced at the trial. There is a statute which makes a seditious conspiracy unlawful. Petitioners, however, were not charged with a "conspiracy to overthrow" the Government.

They were charged with a conspiracy to form a party and groups and assemblies of people who teach and advocate the overthrow of our Government by force or violence and with a conspiracy to advocate and teach its overthrow by force and violence. It may well be that indoctrination in the techniques of terror to destroy the Government would be indictable under either statute. But the teaching which is condemned here is of a different character.

So far as the present record is concerned, what petitioners did was to organize people to teach and themselves teach the Marxist-Leninist doctrine contained chiefly in four books: Foundations of Leninism by Stalin (1924), The Communist Manifesto by Marx and Engels (1848), State and Revolution by Lenin (1917), History of the Communist Party of the Soviet Union (B) (1939).

Those books are to Soviet Communism what Mein Kampf was to Nazism. If they are understood, the ugliness of Communism is revealed, its deceit and cunning are exposed, the nature of its activities becomes apparent, and the chances of its success less likely. That is not, of course, the reason why petitioners chose these books for their classrooms. They are fervent Communists to whom these volumes are gospel. They preached the creed with the hope that some day it would be acted upon.

The opinion of the Court does not outlaw these texts nor condemn them to the fire, as the Communists do literature offensive to their creed. But if the books themselves are not outlawed, if they can lawfully remain on library shelves, by what reasoning does their use in a classroom become a crime? It would not be a crime under the Act to introduce these books to a class, though that would be teaching what the creed of violent overthrow of the government is. The Act, as construed, requires the element of intent — that those who teach the creed believe in it. The crime then depends not on what is taught but on who the teacher is. That is to make freedom of speech turn not on *what is said,* but on the *intent* with which it is said. Once we start down that road we enter territory dangerous to the liberties of every citizen.

There was a time in England when the concept of constructive treason flourished. Men were punished not for raising a hand against the king but for thinking murderous thoughts about him. The Framers of the Constitution were alive to that abuse and took steps to see that the practice would not flourish here. Treason was defined to require overt acts — the evolution of a plot against the country into an actual project. The present case is not one of treason. But the analogy is close when the illegality is made to turn on intent, not on the nature

of the act. We then start probing men's minds for motive and purpose; they become entangled in the law not for what they did but *for what they thought;* they get convicted not for what they said but for the purpose with which they said it.

Intent, of course, often makes the difference in the law. An act otherwise excusable or carrying minor penalties may grow to an abhorrent thing if the evil intent is present. We deal here, however, not with ordinary acts but with speech, to which the Constitution has given a special sanction.

The vice of treating speech as the equivalent of overt acts of a treasonable or seditious character is emphasized by a concurring opinion, which by invoking the law of conspiracy makes speech do service for deeds which are dangerous to society. The doctrine of conspiracy has served divers and oppressive purposes and in its broad reach can be made to do great evil. But never until today has anyone seriously thought that the ancient law of conspiracy could constitutionally be used to turn speech into seditious conduct. Yet that is precisely what is suggested. I repeat that we deal here with speech alone, not with speech *plus* acts of sabotage or unlawful conduct. Not a single seditious act is charged in the indictment. To make a lawful speech unlawful because two men conceive it is to raise the law of conspiracy to appalling proportions. That course is to make a radical break with the past and to violate one of the cardinal principles of our constitutional scheme.

Free speech has occupied an exalted position because of the high service it has given our society. Its protection is essential to the very existence of a democracy. The airing of ideas releases pressures which otherwise might become destructive. When ideas compete in the market for acceptance, full and free discussion exposes the false and they gain few adherents. Full and free discussion even of ideas we hate encourages the testing of our own prejudices and preconceptions. Full and free discussion keeps a society from becoming stagnant and unprepared for the stresses and strains that work to tear all civilizations apart.

Full and free discussion has indeed been the first article of our faith. We have founded our political system on it. It has been the safeguard of every religious, political, philosophical, economic, and racial group amongst us. We have counted on it to keep us from embracing what is cheap and false; we have trusted the common sense of our people to choose the doctrine true to our genius and to reject the rest. This has been the one single outstanding tenet that has made our institutions the symbol of freedom and equality. We have deemed it more costly to liberty to suppress a despised minority than to let them vent their spleen. We have above all else feared the political censor. We have wanted a land where our people can be exposed to all the diverse creeds and cultures of the world.

There comes a time when even speech loses its constitutional immunity. Speech innocuous one year may at another time fan such destructive flames that it must be halted in the interests of the safety of the Republic. That is the meaning of the "clear and present danger" test. When conditions are so critical that there will be no time to avoid the evil that the speech threatens, it is time to call a halt. Otherwise, free speech which is the strength of the Nation will be the cause of its destruction.

Yet free speech is the rule, not the exception. The restraint to be constitutional must be based on more than fear, on more than passionate opposition against the speech, on more than a revolted dislike for its contents. There must be some immediate injury to society that is likely if speech is allowed. . . .

. . . there should be evidence of record on the issue. This record, however, contains no evidence whatsoever showing that the acts charged, *viz.*, the teaching of the Soviet theory of revolution with the hope that it will be realized, have created any clear and present danger to the Nation. The Court, however, rules to the contrary. It says, "The formation by petitioners of such a highly organized conspiracy, with rigidly disciplined members subject to call when the leaders, these petitioners, felt that the time had come for action, coupled with the inflammable nature of world conditions, similar uprisings in other countries, and the touch-and-go nature of our relations with countries with whom petitioners were in the very least ideologically attuned, convince us that their convictions were justified on this score."

That ruling is in my view not responsive to the issue in the case. We might as well say that the speech of petitioners is outlawed because Soviet Russia and her Red Army are a threat to world peace.

The nature of Communism as a force on the world scene would, of course, be relevant to the issue of clear and present danger of petitioners' advocacy within the United States. But the primary consideration is the strength and tactical position of petitioners and their converts in this country. On that there is no evidence in the record. If we are to take judicial notice of the threat of Communists within the nation, it should not be difficult to conclude that as a political party they are of little consequence. Communists in this country have never made a respectable or serious showing in any election. I would doubt that there is a village, let alone a city or county or state which the Communists could carry. Communism in the world scene is no bogey-man; but Communism as a political faction or party in this country plainly is. Communism has been so thoroughly exposed in this country that it has been crippled as a political force. Free speech has destroyed it as an effective political party. It is inconceivable that those who went up and down this country preaching the doctrine of revolution which petitioners espouse would have any success. In days of trouble and confusion when bread lines were long, when the unemployed walked the streets, when people were starving, the advocates of a short-cut by revolution might have a chance to gain adherents. But today there are no such conditions. The country is not in despair; the people know Soviet Communism; the doctrine of Soviet revolution is exposed in all of its ugliness and the American people want none of it.

How it can be said that there is a clear and present danger that this advocacy will succeed is, therefore, a mystery. Some nations less resilient than the United States, where illiteracy is high and where democratic traditions are only budding, might have to take drastic steps and jail these men for merely speaking their creed. But in America they are miserable merchants of unwanted ideas; their wares remain unsold. The fact that their ideas are abhorrent does not make them powerful.

The political impotence of the Communists in this country does not, of course, dispose of the problem. Their numbers; their positions in industry and government; the extent to which they have in fact infiltrated the police, the armed services, transportation, stevedor-

ing, power plants, munitions works, and other critical places — these facts all bear on the likelihood that their advocacy of the Soviet theory of revolution will endanger the Republic. But the record is silent on these facts. If we are to proceed on the basis of judicial notice, it is impossible for me to say that the Communists in this country are so potent or so strategically deployed that they must be suppressed for their speech. I could not so hold unless I were willing to conclude that the activities in recent years of committees of Congress, of the Attorney General, of labor unions, of state legislatures, and of Loyalty Boards were so futile as to leave the country on the edge of grave peril. To believe that petitioners and their following are placed in such critical positions as to endanger the Nation is to believe the incredible. It is safe to say that the followers of the creed of Soviet Communism are known to the F. B. I.; that in case of war with Russia they will be picked up overnight as were all prospective saboteurs at the commencement of World War II; that the invisible army of petitioners is the best known, the most beset, and the least thriving of any fifth column in history. Only those held by fear and panic could think otherwise.

This is my view if we are to act on the basis of judicial notice. But the mere statement of the opposing views indicates how important it is that we know the facts before we act. Neither prejudice nor hate nor senseless fear should be the basis of this solemn act. Free speech — the glory of our system of government — should not be sacrificed on anything less than plain and objective proof of danger that the evil advocated is imminent. On this record no one can say that petitioners and their converts are in such a strategic position as to have even the slightest chance of achieving their aims.

The First Amendment provides that "Congress shall make no law . . . abridging the freedom of speech." The Constitution provides no exception. This does not mean, however, that the Nation need hold its hand until it is in such weakened condition that there is no time to protect itself from incitement to revolution. Seditious conduct can always be punished. But the command of the First Amendment is so clear that we should not allow Congress to call a halt to free speech except in the extreme case of peril from the speech itself. The First Amendment makes confidence in the common sense of our people and in their maturity of judgment the great postulate of our democracy. Its philosophy is that violence is rarely, if ever, stopped by denying civil liberties to those advocating resort to force. The First Amendment reflects the philosophy of Jefferson "that it is time

enough for the rightful purposes of civil government for its officers to interfere when principles break out into overt acts against peace and good order." The political censor has no place in our public debates. Unless and until extreme and necessitous circumstances are shown our aim should be to keep speech unfettered and to allow the processes of law to be invoked only when the provocateurs among us move from speech to action.

Vishinsky wrote in 1948 in The Law of the Soviet State, "In our state, naturally there can be no place for freedom of speech, press, and so on for the foes of socialism."

Our concern should be that we accept no such standard for the United States. Our faith should be that our people will never give support to these advocates of revolution, so long as we remain loyal to the purposes for which our Nation was founded.

Roger S. Abbott:

THE FEDERAL LOYALTY PROGRAM:
Background and Problems

THE broad purpose of the loyalty program enunciated by the [President's Temporary Commission on Employee Loyalty] and adopted in the preamble of the Executive Order is twofold: not only to afford "maximum protection . . . [to] the United States against infil-

tration of disloyal persons into the ranks of its employees," but also to afford "equal protection from unfounded accusations of disloyalty . . . [to] the loyal employees of the Government." To this second official objective may be added, think some observers, the assumption

Roger S. Abbott, "The Federal Loyalty Program: Background and Problems," *American Political Science Review*, XLII, No. 3 (June, 1948). Used by permission.

that the program was undertaken in part to forestall more drastic action against employees by Congress.

Whether or not this belief is correct, the sweeping accusation sometimes heard that the loyalty order is an intentional attack upon the employees' civil liberties appears untenable. Actually, the order proposed the first general and fairly orderly procedure, with provision for appeal, made mandatory as a prerequisite to dismissal on grounds of disloyalty. The possible unintended effects of the program on civil liberties and the quality of the federal service present another question, examined briefly at the conclusion of this article.

The standard of disloyalty set forth in the order consists of the general test that "on all the evidence, reasonable grounds exist for belief that the person involved is disloyal to the government of the United States." Six "activities and associations" may be considered. In brief, these are (1) sabotage and espionage; (2) treason or sedition or advocacy thereof; (3) advocacy of revolution or force to alter the constitutional form of government of the United States; (4) intentional, unauthorized disclosure of confidential documents under circumstances indicating disloyalty; (5) acting so as to serve the interests of another government in preference to the interests of the United States; (6) "membership in, affiliation with, or sympathetic association with any foreign or domestic organization, association . . . designated by the Attorney-General as totalitarian, fascist, communist, or subversive. . . ."

This part of the order has evoked considerable criticism largely focused on the sixth point. Some questions have been raised about the wording of other points which could lead to undesirable and probably unintended interpretation, but limitations of space preclude their analysis here. The opposition to the sixth point has generally centered on the vagueness of the terms, the possible implication of "guilt by association," and the seemingly unrestricted authority assigned to the Attorney-General.

The indefiniteness of the words used is undeniable, and it may be doubted whether specific and completely satisfactory definitions could be evolved for them. A further potential difficulty was seen in the order's failure to indicate that the "sympathetic association" must be with the portion of the organization's program making it "subversive," assuming that some of its objectives might be worthy. Although the language of the order would not necessarily preclude a violation of the fundamental American legal doctrine of punishment only for personal guilt, subsequent official assurances have been given in this connection.

Discussion of the power (or onerous duty) given to the Attorney-General concerning organizations has emphasized that they were not granted open hearings with an opportunity to defend themselves, and that no provision was made for publication of the list of organizations so designated, so as to permit employees to be fully informed as to the government's attitude concerning them.

The former criticism has received no official rebuttal or explanation other than the statement that the Executive Order contains no authorization for hearings. The latter question has been answered. After months of study of voluminous files on more than three hundred organizations by a staff of Justice Department lawyers said to number as many as thirty, Attorney-General Clark finally on November 24, 1947, transmitted a list of designated organizations, as required by the Executive Order, to the chairman of the Loyalty Review Board, who published it on December 4. The Attorney-General explained that the FBI investigative reports were correlated and that memoranda on each organization were prepared and reviewed by the Solicitor-General, the Assistant Attorneys-General, the Assistant Solicitor-General, and by himself.

Notwithstanding this screening process, and the Attorney-General's qualification that it is possible that many loyal persons belong to the groups, the list received considerable comment, some finding it too restricted or too inclusive. The list included 47 groups named in 1943 for reference only by executive agencies; 33 newly designated organizations (including several affiliates of the Communist party and of the Civil Rights Congress); and 11 schools, said to be adjuncts of the Communist party. The accompanying letter noted that the list was neither complete nor final. A number of small and local groups were not included; many were not added because the available information was insufficient. Others, innocuous at the time, might become dangerously infiltrated, and new ones might be formed.

The first legal challenge to this action was made by one of the designated organizations, the Joint Anti-Fascist Refugee Committee. Mr. O. John Rogge filed suit in its behalf in a federal district court in Washington, D. C., in February, 1948, charging that the Executive Order violated due process by depriving the organization of a hearing. It was alleged that the Committee had suffered such damages as loss of tax-exempt status, financial backers, and friends.

The operation and procedures of the loyalty program may now be outlined. The program was not actually started until August, 1947. Additional funds were sought in May after a Budget Bureau study, but Congress did not act on the request until late July. One reason for the delay was the consideration of a bill introduced by Representative Rees to replace the executive program. This measure adopted substantially the same standards as the Executive Order, but altered the procedures in such a way as to arouse doubt by executive officials as to its administrative feasibility and its probable cost. It was passed by the House, but not reported from committee in the Senate.

At the end of July, the executive program was granted $11,000,000, and in August it was begun. The preliminary service-wide check required each of the approximately two million employees to be finger-printed and to answer a short questionnaire, designed only for identification purposes. Contrary to popular impression, it did not involve any attesting of loyalty or disclosure of membership in political organizations. The occasional highlighted refusal to answer has represented, not an attempt at concealment, but a general protest against the program.

The next step was the transmission of these completed questionnaires to the FBI for a file check to determine the existence of "derogatory information." If none is found, there is no further investigation, and the form is returned with such notation to the Civil Service Commission and then forwarded to the employing agency. However, if some data or allegations which might have relevancy to loyalty are revealed, the Bureau then undertakes a "full field investigation" of the individual.

At the outset of the program, it was estimated that approximately two per cent of the names would produce such a question. On March 16, 1948, however, FBI Director Hoover announced that 1,005,944 names had been cleared and that only 777 full investigations had been instituted. Of these, 170 had been completed, resulting in 33 determinations of loyalty and 94 adverse findings.

After such an investigation has been made, the agent's report is subjected to review at several levels within the FBI. If there is an adverse finding and it is approved by the Bureau, the report is sent to the appropriate agency loyalty board, composed of not fewer than three persons. If this board's examination of the report, possibly supplemented by information obtained from the employee, results in an adverse determination, a letter of charges is sent to the employee. This document contains the charges in factual detail "so far as security considerations will permit" and a statement of the employee's right to answer them in writing within ten days and of his right to have an administrative hearing, in which he may appear, be represented by counsel, and present evidence. The hearing is private, and a copy of the transcript of proceedings is furnished to him.

If the finding after hearing is adverse, the employee may be suspended, but he then has the right of further appeal within ten days to the agency head. The latter, or his designee, may fix the scope and extent of the hearing. A third appeal within twenty days after receipt of final decision may be carried to the central Loyalty Review Board. The membership of this Board, authorized by the Executive Order, was announced on November 8, 1947, by the Civil Service Commission after the list of twenty members had been approved by the President. The members are private citizens, meeting from time to time and serving without compensation. The membership was subsequently increased to twenty-three, with a potential total of twenty-five. The Board is representative of a broad cross-section of the public and includes several prominent professors of political science, lawyers, and others. The Board held its first meeting on December 3, resulting in the development of a statement of principles and procedures for itself and for the agency and regional boards, which was issued on December 17.

Appeal to this Board may also be made by an applicant for federal employment after he has had recourse to the appropriate regional loyalty board, created and staffed by the Civil Service Commission in fourteen regions. The procedures are similar to those followed by the agency boards. The name check, instituted for all applicants after September 30, 1947, is conducted by the Civil Service Commission and is required, by the Executive Order, to be made against not only the files of the FBI and of the Commission, but also those of the military intelligence agencies, the House Committee on Un-American Activities, local law-enforcement agencies, schools and colleges of the applicant, his former employers, references given by him, and other appropriate sources.

If "derogatory information" is produced by this check of an estimated 500,000 applicants per year — which might occur in 2.6 per cent of the cases, according to an early Commission estimate — a "full field investigation" is made by the FBI.

The time which will probably be required for adjudication and appeal of such cases is uncertain. With reference to employee appeals, assuming that they are carried to the central board, the maximum time for an individual case has been estimated at ninety days. The handling of all appealed employee cases should be completed by October, 1949. It is believed, however, that few cases — perhaps twenty per cent at the most of those in which there are original adverse determinations — will reach the top level. A large proportion of the cases will probably be "washed out" by the agency boards or heads — that is, the persons will either be cleared or the charges against them may be so convincing that they will not appeal. Thus the major work load may fall on the agency boards. The relatively few cases reaching the top board will be assigned to hearing panels whose decisions may be reviewed by the full board at its discretion.

The central Loyalty Review Board, however, is expected to set the general tone of the loyalty program and, in the words of its chairman, to "do its utmost to see that justice is done, that individual rights are protected as fully as may be." A basic dilemma was presented to it in the fact that the FBI report is vital to the entire program and that the Bureau has stated that if confidential sources are involved, their disclosure would greatly reduce the Bureau's resources. Director Hoover has declared that his agency is charged "more primarily with the security of the country from espionage or sabotage," and that it is necessary to have certain informants who will furnish data of very secret character whose disclosure would be detrimental to such security. Such sources he will not identify. Two other types of informants, he has stated, can be revealed. These are the "contact type" (who may be a lawyer, Congressman, or prominent business man) and the "next-door neighbor or fellow employee." Even in such instances, however, the informants' identity could be revealed only upon the basis of their previous consent. If such were sought,

he doubts whether much information could be obtained. Nevertheless, the possibility of personal grudges and malicious rumor should be considered.

According to the original view of the chairman of the Board, it will probably not be practicable to permit cross-examination "in the great majority of cases." On the other hand, it is said that a FBI representative will be available to evaluate for the hearing board the reliability of the confidential source. Furthermore, the disadvantage to the employee of non-confrontation of witnesses will be considered in the adjudication. An additionally stated justification of this policy is that, legally, the government is entitled to discharge any employee for reasons which seem sufficient to it and without granting any hearing.

Although technically the constitutional guarantee of confrontation in criminal prosecutions does not apply, the case for its use presented "grave considerations" to the Board. Serious critics, while accepting the FBI explanation, have suggested that although confidential informants may be used in the investigation, the record used by the board could be restricted to the testimony of those who could be confronted and examined — a procedure somewhat comparable to that necessarily used in some narcotics, sedition, and immigration prosecutions, even though conviction may be rendered more difficult.

A more fundamental rebuttal is made to the point that government employment is a privilege rather than a right. The possible consequences of a finding of "disloyalty," or perhaps even of an unfounded allegation thereof, on the individual's future employment prospects — private as well as public — and on his reputation cannot be overemphasized. . . .

L. A. Nikolorić:

THE GOVERNMENT LOYALTY PROGRAM

ESTABLISHED by the President's Executive Order 9835 in March, 1947, the government's loyalty program moves into its fourth year. The program presents a complex problem: whether, in the name of "loyalty" and "national security," our society is justified in abusing most of the basic tenets of Anglo-American jurisprudence and legal philosophy traditional since the seventeenth century.

The purpose of the program is not to discharge employees expressly because of what they have done in the past. President Truman has stated that it is aimed at "potentially disloyal" persons who, because of attitudes and ideas they entertain today or subscribed to yesterday, might in the future undertake action contrary to the best interests of the United States. The basic concept of the program — to ferret out the "potentially disloyal"— violates a most important principle of Anglo-American law: that one cannot be punished for merely considering the commission of a crime, or for thinking in such a way that a body determines that one might undertake action contrary to the law.

The program also violates judicial safeguards against punishment which are traditional in free societies. The rights to have a reasonable notice of charges, to cross-examine and confront one's accusers, to judicial review before punishment is meted out, to be judged by an impartial tribunal — these are, among others, eliminated from the program.

The loyalty program also distorts the concept of equal justice under the law. It assumes that a democratic government may exact from its employees special standards of conduct wholly offensive to constitutional guarantees of freedom and justice as applied to ordinary citizens. We deny two and a half million government employees political and intellectual freedoms in order to protect ourselves from the potentially subversive.

These innovations are spreading not only to some three and a half million state and local employees (the County of Los Angeles, among other local governments, has instituted a loyalty check), but elsewhere. The AFL and the CIO have undertaken to purge the Communists. The Army, the Navy and the Air Force pass on the loyalty of the employees of private contractors who bid successfully on government jobs having to do with classified material. Congressmen have urged that all employees working for industries connected with the national security be subjected to a similar screening. Presumably this concerns the various utilities — in steel, automobile, transportation and others. Teachers and scientists have been discharged for entertaining unpopular ideas. Even veterans' organizations have pledged themselves to loyalty programs. The most liberal of these, the American Veterans Committee, has adopted resolutions directing its officers to purge the Communists.

Since we are rapidly accepting the

From the *American Scholar*, XIX (Summer, 1950). Copyright of United Chapters of Phi Beta Kappa. Used by permission.

proposition that American institutions have a right to examine their membership on the basis of their "loyalty," it is appropriate to determine what the government's loyalty program is and how it operates, its ideology, and the concrete effects of its operation. . . .

The discovery of the potentially disloyal is no easy task. Executive Order 9835 directs the Boards to take action if

. . . on the basis of all the evidence, reasonable grounds exist for belief that the person involved is disloyal.

It is, therefore, the duty of the Boards to determine the existence of a nebulous state of mind which might lead an employee to commit in the future a disloyal act, either willfully or through an indiscretion. The most important elements of consideration are of necessity the employee's political beliefs, the organizations to which he has belonged, and the associations he has had.

Experience proves that it is not necessary for the employee to have been a member of either a Communist or Fascist organization. He will be found wanting if he has been "sympathetic" to communism or fascism, friendly to persons or organizations that are sympathetic, associated with such persons or organizations, or even "unduly talkative" in the presence of persons who are associated with sympathetic persons. The Boards do not find it necessary to prove any of these matters. They are required only to find "a reasonable doubt."

In order to assist the Boards, the Attorney General, in December, 1947, and by various supplements, designated some 150 organizations — membership in or sympathy for which is held to be indicative of disloyalty. These lists were promulgated without hearings. No explana-tion for the inclusion of any organization was given.

The procedural safeguards fundamental to a fair trial or hearing have been spelled out on many occasions by the Supreme Court. These standards[1] are:

1. There must be an impartial judge or jury.
2. The accused must be permitted representation by counsel.
3. The charges must be clear and stated with particularity so that the accused is clearly informed.
4. The law which the accused is alleged to have broken must have been passed before he committed the act.
5. There must be confrontation of the accusers and the right of cross-examination.
6. The accused is protected against self-incrimination.
7. There may be no double-jeopardy.
8. There may be no cruel or unusual punishment.

Such safeguards are not available to an employee charged with potential disloyalty. The generalities employed in loyalty charges are demonstrated by a typical example:

You are charged with having associated with Communists or with persons or organizations in sympathy with communism.

Although the order provides that the employee is entitled to a charge stating the offense with some particularity, this is limited by the discretion of the agency in the interest of security considerations. Practice has shown that it has been almost impossible for an employee or his lawyer to secure a full or complete statement of the offenses.

Defending against such charges is diffi-

[1] Taken from *U. S. v. Lovett* (1946), opinion of Mr. Justice Black.

cult. The burden is placed on the employee to recall all the persons with whom, and organizations with which, he has ever been in contact, and to explain them. He must also prove affirmatively that he adheres to certain nebulous standards that might be construed by the Board as indicative of so loyal a state of mind that the employee will never commit a disloyal act.

The following quotation demonstrates the position in which an employee finds himself. In this case, Mr. A was faced with an unexplained action of the State Department in dismissing him "for security reasons." A asked the Board to tell him what he had done to justify the action, so that he might defend himself. The Board representative said:

Well, we realize the difficulty you are in, in this position; on the other hand, I'd suggest that you might think back over your own career and perhaps in your own mind delve into some of the factors that have gone into your career which you think might have been subject to question and see what they are and see whether you'd like to explain or make any statement with regard to any of them. . . .

The case of B is also typical. B was charged with "associating with persons in sympathy with communism." B's lawyer asked the department Board for a list of the persons. The department gave the names of three persons — of whom B knew only one, and him slightly. Counsel made an additional request and received six more names, of which B did know two. At the hearing B was met with four more names and was unprepared to make an adequate defense.

Even when names and organizations are specified, the employee is not told what is wrong with the alleged associate. Again defense is difficult. The process which ties in the accused with the associate is also used to tar the associate. For example, C was charged with associating with ten persons. C was closely associated with only one of them. Not only was C faced with the job of clearing himself, but in order to "purify" his association, found it necesary also to present long testimony in his associate's behalf.

In this connection, even the Boards themselves are not told by the FBI the source of derogatory information. It is, therefore, impossible even for them to weigh the evidence. This is revealed by the hearing of D before a Board at the Brooklyn Navy Yard. The FBI had designated its informants to the Board by symbols, "T-1, T-2, etc."

The following colloquy took place:

Board Member: Did you ever act as an organizer for the Communist Party or attempt to recruit others?

D: No.

B M: [It] has been corroborated, checked and verified —

Attorney for D: By whom?

B M: I can't tell you. . . . We don't even know who the accuser is.

Nor are the accusations made under oath. The following took place during an appeal hearing before the Review Board. In reply to counsel's questions, asking whether the statements of the accusers were sworn, and also the identity of the accusers, the Chairman replied:

I don't think so. . . . I haven't the slightest knowledge as to who they were. . . .

The employee is not tried by an impartial judge. The Board accusing him conducts the inquiry, questions the employee, and renders judgment.

There is no confrontation of the persons who have given derogatory reports to the FBI. Nor has the employee any right to cross-examine the informer. These rights are denied under the theory that they might dry up sources of information. The Chairman of the Review Board, Mr. Seth Richardson, has stated:

We have concluded that the objection to no confrontation and no cross-examination, which are important, is not essentially controlling.

Examples of double jeopardy occur when a provisional employee (over whom the Civil Service Commission has concurrent jurisdiction with the employing agency) is charged with disloyalty. For example, E was charged and cleared by a Civil Service Commission Board. Thereafter, the Army, by whom E was employed, instituted new proceedings on the same charges.

The proper presentation of an appeal is complicated by the order's requirement that Boards "shall state merely the action taken." It is impossible to tell what evidence the Board relied on, what findings of fact it made (other than the result), or even if all of its evidence was revealed to the employee. For that reason, there is no way to specify in what respects the lower Board was in error.

None of these things could happen in any other court or board proceeding directed against an individual in the United States. Axis Sally and Judith Coplon, who were charged with overt acts of treason and espionage, have received more procedural protection than is accorded the potentially disloyal. A common pickpocket may insist on every traditional and fundamental safeguard. A government employee may not. No one would dream of indicting Axis Sally for merely contemplating broadcasting Nazi propaganda; we would not consider putting a petty thief in jail for thinking

about picking his neighbor's pocket. Yet we discharge and publicly smear government employees who have done nothing wrongful, who may not consider committing an act of disloyalty. We fire them because, on the basis of standards of the status quo, the Board suspects that they might do so in the future.

Those who would defend the program argue that the government is not required to secure to its employees procedural safeguards when it fires them. It is said that no citizen has an inherent right to government employment. Thus the government may fire arbitrarily – because it does not like the color of the employee's hair, because he is inefficient, or because the government fears that the employee may become a security risk. The procedural safeguards that are provided – charges and a hearing – are a matter of the sovereign's largess. They do not accrue to the employee as a matter of constitutional right. Therefore, the employee may not ask for other safeguards as a matter of constitutional right.

The opponents have a convincing case. Many judges, notably Mr. Justice Black, have argued that once having been hired, a government employee does secure a vested interest in his job which shall not be taken from him without cause. Cause may not be a matter of speculation; it must be a reality – such as inefficiency or overt acts of disloyalty.

Furthermore, a dismissal for disloyalty entails a permanent brand amounting to treason. Experience has shown that an employee who has been discharged under the loyalty program is unable to get another job; his career is ruined; he loses the respect of the community. Dismissal on loyalty or security grounds transcends the arbitrary right to fire. It amounts to punishment by government, which is protected by the Constitution. If this be the case, an employee who is fired on these grounds does have the constitutional right to traditional due process and safeguards.

Regardless of the coldly legal interpretation of the situation, it is obvious that a loyalty proceeding is a serious matter. On moral grounds, the government should not ruin an employee's career on a conjectural determination that he may in the future become disloyal. It must be remembered that the loyalty program was not designed or intended to punish people who have committed overt acts of disloyalty or treason. Not an employee fired has been charged with the commission of a wrongful act. During a recent public discussion with me, Mr. Seth Richardson, Chairman of the Loyalty Review Board, stated that the loyalty program has not discovered a single instance of espionage or any other overt action contrary to the best interests of the United States.

There are innumerable statutes calculated to deal with persons who are or have been acting contrary to our best interests. They include sanctions against espionage, sabotage, treason or advocacy of the overthrow of the government by force. More important to the inquiry here, any government agency may fire an employee for cause. "Cause" includes everything from simple inefficiency to disagreement with the agency's policy. Every applicant for government employment must sign, under oath, a statement that he does not subscribe to subversive doctrines and does not belong to any organization that does. Failure to make full disclosure is punishable as a criminal offense.

If we are to commit ourselves to a program that is (at least in moral, and probably in constitutional terms) repugnant to traditional jurisprudence, it is only fair to evaluate the reasons for calling such a program into being, the resulting ideology, and the results in practical terms.

The program was instituted for two major reasons. The first was political. In March, 1947, when the order was signed, the future of the Democratic Party was not bright. One of the principal issues on which the Republicans had won the off-year election of 1946 was that the Administration had been lax in permitting spies and subversives to infiltrate into government. It became politically expedient for the Democrats to take positive steps to appear diligent in the matter of Communists.

The second reason is the more important. It is our fear of Russia and the ideology of communism. The War left Russia the only power capable of arguing with our new role in world leadership. We are afraid of Russia's military power and fearful of the consequences to society as a whole in the event of a test of strength employing frightening new weapons. We therefore justify stringent methods to root out of government actual or potential Communist agents and spies.

Perhaps even more important (we have before been faced with threatening world powers) is our fear of the Communist ideology. The Communists have promised the world that capitalism will collapse of its own weight and inefficiencies. England, France and other traditionally capitalist countries are making concessions to various government controls. We are doing the same thing. Even in great prosperity, our governmental and private economic bureaucracies, unwieldy and frozen, are unable to feed, clothe and house our people with relative adequacy. The prediction of the Communists makes us uneasy. This is particularly true because we have come to think of Communists as supermen —

more clever and efficient than we. In spite of the fact that communism has never been more unpopular in America, we have never been more apprehensive of the scrubby little group of fanatics who straggle up Eighth Avenue in New York on May Day.

These fears are not clearly defined. We are suspicious of change. Confusion is added from the semantic designation of both communism and so-called liberalism as "left-wing." To many the two are synonymous. Hence, to find a potentially disloyal American, find a man who expresses dissatisfaction with the established order of things — a man who believes in racial equality, socialized medicine, labor unions, equalization of economic opportunity, or increased government activity in economic affairs — particularly if the believer is not of Anglo-American stock. These things are "left-wing"; so is communism. A *fortiori*, a man who believes in them may become in the future a Communist agent.

Witness the following excerpts from transcripts of various Boards:

1. Q. Was your father native born?
A. Yes.
Q. How about his father?
A. Yes.
Q. Your mother, was she native born?
A. Yes.
Q. How about her parents?
A. Yes.
2. Q. Have you ever had Negroes in your home?
3. Q. How large a unit do you have supervision over?
A. Approximately twenty people right now.
Q. Any difference in color?
A. Not at the present time . . . all white. We have had a colored man in other years.
Q. Professional or clerical?
A. Professional.

4. Q. Are you in favor of the Marshall Plan?
5. Q. There is a suspicion in the record that you are in sympathy with the underprivileged. Is this true?
6. Q. Did you see X soliciting funds for strikers?
7. Q. In your recollection, do you recall ever discussing any topic which might be sympathetic to Communist doctrine?
A. Yes.
Q. Would you care to state what it was and who it was made to?
A. I have been sick for years, and so I have discussed what they call nationalized medicine.
8. Q. Did you ever hear any political discussions at X's home?
9. Q. Did you ever attend any political forums at X's home?
10. Q. Are your friends and associates intelligent, clever?
11. Q. When did you become a member of the Communist Party?
A. I never became a member of the Communist Party.
Q. If you are, as you say, a loyal American, why do you persist in denying that you were a member of the Communist Party?

In fairness, it must be stated that these questions are taken out of context. This does not, however, disprove the obvious interest of the Boards in these matters. In every hearing I have attended, these or similar questions have been asked. These questions are not unusual or the exception; they are routine. The point is that the subject matter of this type of inquiry is completely relevant if the purpose of the program to ferret out the potentially disloyal is kept in mind. There is no other way to make a judgment of *potential* disloyalty than to examine a man's associations and attitudes toward matters of controversy, to determine whether that man is wedded to the established order of things or will work toward change.

Thus the potentially disloyal of necessity becomes the non-conformist. The following cases are typical. All were thought worthy of Board action. No effort has been made to pick out "dramatic" examples. Each one is routine; those in which the employee was dismissed are indicated.

In 1942 F was a history student and became interested in Communist philosophy and method. For a period of some four weeks F attended a few cell meetings in his college town. He does not recall whether he signed any petitions or other papers, but may have made a contribution of approximately a dollar and a half. He rejected what he found, and since then has been, if anything, anti-Communist. He is active in the Americans for Democratic Action, an organization which is outspoken in its opposition to communism. He belongs to no other political organizations. Since this period of four weeks, eight years ago, this man has never associated with Communists or expressed any sympathy for the doctrine. No other charges were made. F was discharged.

G is a woman who was born in Russia. During the Revolution she escaped and has never returned. Her mother and father were shot by the Communists; her brother "disappeared" in Siberia. G was charged with undue sympathy for Russia. Although no other evidence or reason appears in the transcript of G's hearing, she was fired.

H was a civilian employee in Japan. A conference was held to discuss ways to break up a black market in agricultural products. H suggested as a solution that, in distributing fertilizers to farmers, it be required that the farmers market a certain percentage of their produce through occupation authorities. The senior officer at the conference accused H of being a Communist, since the suggestion sounded as though he were opposed to free enterprise. Shortly thereafter, the employee was relieved and sent back to the United States to defend a loyalty charge because of this incident.

I was charged with disloyalty because an associate reported to an FBI agent that his mother-in-law was pro-Russian.

J was charged because it was reported that he had been "critical" of the policies of our Ambassador to Russia.

K is a scientist who had an acquaintance in college whom he had not seen for over fifteen years. The acquaintance was named a defendant in a proceeding involving alleged Communists. In answer to an appeal made to most of his classmates, K contributed some money to his friend's defense. Although this acquaintance was fully acquitted, K was charged with disloyalty. The agency board found against K, but was reversed on appeal.

Miss L spent one afternoon collecting money for Russian War Relief in front of a movie house. She also was instrumental in having Senators Ball and Pepper talk to the people of her city concerning the necessity of accepting Russia as an ally. These events took place in 1943, when the Russians were bearing much of the brunt of the war. Miss L also did Red Cross work, collected money and knitted sweaters for British, French and Russian War Relief. Since the war, she has frequently expressed herself as an anti-Communist and as favoring such Communist-denounced programs as the Marshall Plan and Universal Military Training. She was charged on these facts as being disloyal.

M married a girl who, ten years before, as a sophomore in college, had been a member of the Young Communist

League. The YCL in her school was almost exclusively interested in low-cost dormitory facilities and in higher pay for scholarship jobs. Mrs. M resigned from the YCL after six or eight months, and it was not alleged that she since has been in any way connected with communism. Charges were filed against M.

Not included in these examples is a tremendous number of cases involving mistaken identity. These are important to document slipshod methods to which the underlying fears and ideology have driven the Boards and the FBI. This is an example of the kind that occurs with alarming frequency:

N was accused of being a member, along with his wife, of a Communist cell in the Bronx, New York, in 1934. N was not married in 1934; has never been in the Bronx, New York; and, in fact, was not even in the United States in 1934.

An analogous case showing slipshod investigation involves another employee who had been a member of a veterans' organization in the early 1920's. His Post Commander ordered him to "infiltrate" the Workers Alliance to see how the Communists operated. The employee did so and filed a lengthy report, for which he received a commendation. Twenty-five years later, he was charged with disloyalty because of his association with the Alliance.

These cases indicate that the program has accomplished little in the way of security. Figures issued by the Review Board prove this. Ninety-seven persons, out of about two and a half million employees investigated, have been discharged on loyalty grounds. In only 2,037 cases have the Boards found — on their own standards — facts sufficient to justify the kind of charges described above. Of the ninety-seven persons discharged, not a single one has done any-

thing to warrant the interest of the Department of Justice. In no case has a criminal proceeding for espionage, treason or any lesser act of disloyalty been instituted.

A troublesome question is whether the loyalty program should be retained in the so-called "sensitive" agencies — the Atomic Energy Commission, the Department of Defense, and the State Department. Dr. Klaus Fuchs has done much for the proponents of the argument that in these areas, at least, we must examine employees for potential disloyalty because of the greater dangers involved.

My own view is a minority one. The proponents of the "sensitive agency" argument assume that this program is capable of catching the potentially disloyal. Even if we had the necessary instruments to accomplish this, I believe that if free institutions are to survive, they cannot be compromised in this way. A citizen in the Atomic Energy Commission should not be subjected to arbitrary treatment merely because his contribution is the more sensitive. Once the scientist or State Department official becomes a second class citizen, he will not be alone in this classification for long; he will be joined by the employee who deals in foreign trade and commerce, the expert whose concern is labor in the defense industries, and government men who deal with education and health — all fields fertile for sabotage or infiltration.

But the record speaks for itself. The loyalty program has proved to be a miserable failure as far as security is concerned. It has found no spies or security violations in sensitive areas or otherwise. Nor is it geared to; it is geared to accomplish the impossible — determine who tomorrow's spies will be. Let the FBI attend to the business of sabotage and espionage on the basis of the actual, not the potential — on the basis of acts, not possibilities. Let every agency continue to screen applicants for employment carefully; but let us not, in our fear of the police state, compromise free institutions.

The atmosphere in government is one of fear — fear of ideas and of irresponsible and unknown informers. Government employees are afraid to attend meetings of politically minded groups; they are afraid to read "liberal" publications; they screen their friends carefully for "left-wing" ideas. Government employees are in very real danger of dying intellectually and politically. Everyone knows of someone who has been accused of disloyalty — and it amounts to an accusation of treason — on ridiculous charges. Nobody wants to go through a lengthy "loyalty" investigation. The inclination and inevitable result are simply to restrict one's own freedoms.

All Americans suffer thereby. Political growth and progressive evolution depend on a vital and enthusiastic corps of government workers. Democracy can survive only upon the condition of a constant flexibility in its institutions to meet growing social and economic needs. Good government incorporates varying shades of opinion into a synthesis of action in behalf of the greatest good. Synthesis and flexibility are impossible when dissenters or the unorthodox are ruthlessly stamped out. The suppression of opposition can only mean the retention of outmoded and useless institutions, the impossibility of compromise and adjustment.

History has demonstrated again and again that freedom and the maturity of democratic processes cannot survive when the politically and economically dominant suspend traditional safeguards to the unorthodox. This is true, regardless of whether the suspension is undertaken because of fear of outside forces, or whether it is because a society has frozen in its evolutionary progress toward the fuller dignity of man. Surely it cannot be said that the United States, entering into a period of world leadership and enjoying the greatest prosperity in our history, has ceased growing. Let us not through hysteria and the uncertainty engendered by new responsibilities abdicate the basic standards of freedom which made us great. This is what we have done in the government's loyalty program; and this is what we threaten to do in the extension of that program to other segments of our society.

Morris L. Ernst:

SOME AFFIRMATIVE SUGGESTIONS
FOR A LOYALTY PROGRAM

WE have had an ample amount of hysteria in regard to the Loyalty Program. Much of it has been caused by a lack of concern about facts; hysteria usually develops from ignorance. The statistical facts are simple. Congress decided to remove from Civil Service at "the exit end" the Department of Defense, the State Department and the Atomic Energy Commission. In other words, in these areas a person may now lawfully be fired under mandate of Congress without any accusation and without any hearing. It is interesting to note that many who were top officials in the Roosevelt administration have indicated that they are in favor of abolishing Civil Service at the exit end in all departments, for all employees in sensitive areas, or in fact, all employees in important positions. This has long been urged regardless of the factor of security or loyalty, and has been supported by worthy citizens as a measure to improve the service in various large government departments. True enough, it has the capacity of resulting in a spoils system.

Congress voted money so that the FBI could make reports on the two and one-half million government employees operating in other agencies in the government. Under the Atomic Energy Act, the FBI also reports on employees. The latest figures indicate that there was no evidence of hysteria on the part of the FBI.

It did its job as ordered, and, interestingly enough, decided up to May 5, 1950, that only about 11,813 employees of the two and one-half million merited full investigation. The balance of about 2,490,000 were found to have a record that raised no question of division of loyalty. Of the 11,813 the public is apparently ignorant of the fact that the Civil Service Commission as of March 31, 1950, reports that only 202 were severed from service as a result of the President's Loyalty Order. As a footnote to show the extent of the protections provided, we should remember that the Civil Service Loyalty Review Boards reversed findings of potential disloyalty in 143 cases. As another footnote, it might be stated that 1,406 left the service during investigations and 1,028 left prior to adjudications by the Loyalty Hearing Boards. Such severances may have resulted from a consciousness of guilt or have occurred for reasons entirely irrelevant to any question of loyalty.

In brief, numerically the proceedings were carried on in such an orderly fashion that some day, if some Communists are found in sensitive spots, there may develop an hysterical movement to fire Hoover and the Review Boards because they allowed a few to seep through.

I have not much sympathy for the worthy liberals who merely shout down the Loyalty Program and who fail to offer a constructive suggestion about its operation or about a machinery to replace it. There were at the start, according to the not too reliable press, quite a few cases outrageously tried — where the rights of individuals, it seemed to me, were not properly protected. Students of the situation have recently come to the conclusion that the imperfections in the hearings in some of the early cases were cured, or at least substantially improved, in later cases.

Let's wake up. We are facing an utterly new problem in American life. For a century and a half this nation has had to cope with individual behavior patterns involving government employees who had a division of loyalty involving another sovereignty. If today we had only to face the fact that there are more such individuals behaving in disloyal fashion, we would not need any new or additional loyalty protective programs. The old-fashioned spy, who used to bribe the stenographer or fall in love with the boss, is easy to cope with. But we are at war. It is a good war. Unfortunately, it is called a cold war. In my opinion it is a hot war, a non-shooting war. It is a war for the minds of men, and we can lose it without losing a life. Communist dictatorship has never been attained through a vote of a majority of the people ultimately to be squeezed into intellectual starvation. What we are facing are the new dangers derived from secret organized efforts of dictatorships. We must cope with a new kind of organized stealth and anonymity. It is not easy to devise machinery to handle organized sneaks. The avowed Communist is no problem compared to the thousands who are crypto-Communists — who deny that they are Communists. Heywood Broun used to say: "People call me a Communist. I say I am not a Communist. They don't believe me. They are right not to believe me, because they know if I were a Communist I would swear I am not a Communist."

In brief, no one would believe the head of the Communist party under oath. And so we are faced with a difficulty of proof, since in the final analysis the normal way to prove that a person is or is not a Communist is to subpoena the head of the movement and the membership records — both of which no one would trust. It is this *secret* movement which no doubt impelled the President's executive order. The Attorney General prepared a list of organizations which in his opinion contained the roots of "subversive" elements. The simplest approach to this phase of the problem is to remember that "to subvert" means "to turn under" and that the organizations on the Attorney General's list had "turned themselves under." For my part, I was shocked that the list was published without hearings. However, after the publication, the Attorney General announced that any organization could come into his office for a hearing. So far as I know, such proffer of conference was not fully accepted by any single organization on the list. My examination of the list indicates that not a single one of the organizations has ever made full disclosure to the American people. This is the root of the problem and the root of the evil.

Through such secret organizations, decent Americans have been placed in an area of doubt from which it was difficult to remove themselves, since the Communist party obviously thrives on tainting democracy and is unconcerned with injury done to non-Communists. The more the wild and stupid press and some members of Congress improperly label people as subversive or Communist, the happier the Communist party is. If I had my way, I would provide a list of politically active organizations to be compiled *after hearings,* and would only put on the list organizations which have failed to make full disclosure of finances, membership, officers and activities. The United States Supreme Court has upheld as constitutional the drawing of a line between secret benevolent societies or college fraternities, on the one hand, and the Klan, on the other. This in relation to the New York statute calling for Klan disclosure. The answer to our basic dilemma is disclosure rather than suppression, and I am in full accord with the position taken by J. Edgar Hoover, who has repeatedly indicated his opposition to the outlawry of the Communist party. We must all know that we cannot outlaw anything more than a name, and that if the Communist party is outlawed, it may well bob up under a new name such as the "American Peglerites" or some other respectable title. I would go further; I would provide that an organization on the list should have a right to purge itself on making disclosure.

I would then limit the impact of a loyalty or security program to those who have relationships to secret groups, and I would have individual behavior patterns handled as we have done over the past century and a half, without relationship to the new loyalty or security program.

As to the trials of individuals where the proof would rest primarily on relationships to secret underground organizations, I would allow the fullest latitude to the review boards, since we have to pinprick our way into the degree of intimacy of relationship which would raise a question of division of loyalty. It might be money contributions; it might be official activity; on the other hand, it might be the most innocent kind of a well-motivated desire to join in what was

deemed to be non-subversive activities. Most of the people who joined the organizations on the Attorney General's list were no doubt mere suckers, and above all, careless with their names and reputations. Many of them, if asked to endorse a toothpaste, would have applied greater scrutiny than when they were asked to endorse the most precious commodity known to man — ideas. I would go further and provide that an individual could purge himself. There is no such thing in life as sinning without repentance and possible salvation. Stupidly enough, we prevent people from getting out of the Communist party. It is my best judgment that a third of the members of the Communist party under thirty years of age would get out if it were not for the social and economic ostracism presently existing in our culture. To be sure, the Communist party keeps many of them prisoners through blackmail by notifying employers as to ex-Communists, provided the ex-Communist has publicly announced his divorce from that evil movement. But under a decent loyalty program, an individual should always be free to step up to the counter and say: I joined that movement and now, since I have thought it over and since I know that it is a band of uncourageous sneaks, I am withdrawing. Whether the Board believes the particular employee or not would be a question for proof in each case.

I would go further, and provide that the hearings should be either public or private, according to the request of the employee. I would add that, if an employee has been absolved, an announcement should be issued — if *he* so request.

But above all, it is important that the loyalty program be limited to sensitive jobs. I should imagine that 90 per cent of all the jobs in the United States raise no security or loyalty questions. I would not have a Communist in my law office, since the practice of the law involves trust of other people's secrets. No sane person would have a Communist work in sensitive areas of the Atomic Energy Commission. Hence, a fundamental improvement in the situation could be accomplished by a clearer definition within each department, bureau or agency of the areas which are sensitive. This may require considerable reshuffling. The definition of "sensitivity" will mean the development of standards and definitions. I understand that, in one bureau, over a hundred spots were originally declared to be sensitive. On re-examination, plus reshuffling of scrub women, changing of locks on doors and the like, the number was reduced to about twenty. The definition of sensitive areas in itself would greatly simplify the problem, and certainly reduce the work involved. Many a person unemployable in a sensitive job might well be shifted, as is done in England, to non-sensitive areas. I would not want a person of even a potential division of loyalty to be employed cleaning out the trash baskets at the White House, but I should imagine no one would object if such a person were given a job picking up leaves in a public park in Washington. With the limitation of the entire program to sensitive jobs in sensitive agencies, a further improvement might be made — the advent of a realization that no one has a right to a government job, and that, in this great war with dictatorships, the first duty of a government employee is to protect the sovereignty of the state.

Many of my liberal friends have opposed the creation and activities of the review boards. I am violently in favor of them, and I think they have done an efficient and selfless job. It will be inter-esting to see if the conclusions reached by the group studying this matter for one of the big foundations will not soon come out with a finding to the same effect. The reason that I favor outside review boards — that is, boards composed of persons not in the professional employ of the government — is that such persons are further removed from contact with Congress, and hence may produce an additional bit of courage. With Congress what it is, the head of an agency might lean backward to protect himself, whereas the outside review board, not having to go to Congress for appropriations and the like, would be more inclined to look with greater objectivity on the evidence.

I cannot in this brief article outline every detail of what I conceive to be necessary for an ideal loyalty program, but there is one further aspect of any such program which must be mentioned.

I have followed the FBI with great care for many years. I started with a basic human suspicion of all constabularies. In my judgment, the FBI is the single greatest police force in the world, and I am happy to say that Roger Baldwin, the great driving force of the American Civil Liberties Union for many years, has said, with respect to its over-all activities: "It seems to me that your Bureau has accomplished an exceedingly difficult task with rare judicial sense." Any loyalty program must depend on reports. The FBI is a reporting agency. It has no power to hire or fire anyone, except its own employees. It is the duty of the FBI to turn over *all* facts to the employing agencies. Some worthy liberals at one time urged that the FBI files should be screened. It is no doubt true that there is much in the files of the FBI that is either anonymous or is a pick-up of alleged facts uttered by all kinds of persons, reliable or unreliable. Some people urge that the FBI files should be deleted of all such so-called gossip material. This, in my opinion, would be a greater danger than any conceivable loyalty program. If the reporting agency is ever in a position to take a single document out of this file, it will have the power to make anyone either an angel or a devil. The FBI should continue, as in the past, to turn over *all* the information it gets. The employer (that is, the government agency) should take the information and review it — and the heads of government departments are paid to be tough enough to disregard evidence that they think is immaterial, or irrelevant, or unworthy of credence. I also want the FBI to continue to receive anonymous communications or information from sources which have made anonymity a condition of the transmission. The files of the FBI would be greatly weakened if anonymous telephone calls or confidential communications were rejected. Many of the most important jobs done by the FBI were no doubt brought into being by an original tip from a person who did not care to be involved at a hearing or a court trial. The FBI should, if a reporting agency desires it, evaluate the source when the informant wants his identity withheld. It could indicate, for example, that such information came from a sick old woman or from a lawyer of repute of, say, twenty years' standing. As I understand it, the FBI offered, in the loyalty field, either to remove all communications from confidential sources or to evaluate them where possible. The Civil Service Loyalty Board naturally chose the latter course.

In the last analysis the single greatest difficulty comes from the fact that in many situations the reporting agency is in no position to divulge the source of its information: this, because either the informant has not given his name, because he has only given the information on condition that he remain anonymous, or because the divulging of the source would destroy this source as a means of getting other and even more valuable information.

I am not sure that I know exactly how to handle this phase of the dilemma. It may be that the Appeal Board should, in each such instance, declare that it has examined the situation, and that in its opinion the undivulged source has been weighed in the light of the evaluation of the material supplied by the reporting agency. It is this final dilemma that has driven many people to urge the right of free discharge of all employees in sensitive jobs — free in the sense that there be no need for any hearing.

My own feeling, however, is that the entire Loyalty Program arises from the inability of our society to come to grips with anonymous secret groups. The President's Committee on Civil Rights came out unanimously in favor of disclosure by organized groups in our society. I have long been in favor of such a measure. We are operating under a Bill of Rights, which guarantees freedom to speak or not to speak. In my opinion, to the extent that we say to our people: you can either be sneaks or you can stand up publicly, say what you think and be defended — we do encourage the development of further stealth. We now have legislation for disclosure as to magazines and newspapers, disclosure under SEC regulations, the Pure Food and Drug Act, and disclosure as to lobbying. I am not concerned with disclosure of the speaker or writer, because he is always disclosed, but I want to know for whom he is speaking, or for whom he is writing. The great Negro organizations and the spokesmen for the two great labor organizations have come out in favor of disclosure.

It cost $50,000 to run the picket line at the White House up to the time that Hitler attacked Stalin. I would defend the right of the pickets, but I think the public has a right to know for whom they were picketing — who put up the money? I was told that a million dollars was collected by the Communists in the Scottsboro case. I have looked into the matter, and I am convinced that not over $60,000 was spent directly in the defense of the case, which Judge Leibowitz carried on without compensation or reimbursements. What happened to the other $940,000?

The lowest estimate I have received as to the amount of money which will be raised in the defense of the eleven convicted Communists and their attorneys is two million dollars. They have a right to raise that amount of money. Haven't we the right, as a people, to an accounting? My theory as to disclosure is not one limited to Communists. It relates to all substantial organized efforts. I have seen the list of fifty people who gave from $5000 to $50,000 apiece to Gerald L. K. Smith. I would defend the right of Gerald L. K. Smith to send his evil literature through the mails, but I submit that disclosure of the names of the persons for whom Gerald L. K. Smith was speaking is part of the democratic function, where a government's main duty is disclosure and not suppression.

The Loyalty Program, or, as it might be called, the Security Program, will bother us as long as we fail to come to grips with this new element facing our culture — mass organized groups working with vast funds to get to the minds

of our people. If the loyalty proceedings, with all of its defects, has done nothing else, it has no doubt brought to the attention of careless suckers the need for realizing that their names have value, and that they should not join organizations which refuse to make disclosure. To be sure, under a dictatorship, secrecy and stealth are necessary for minority points of view, but in this country, conducting its great and successful experiment in the direction of a free market place of thought, we cannot believe any longer that truth will win out in the market place if the market place is corrupted by the pumping in of ideas in pamphlet or other form with no one knowing who the backers of the ideas are. I should imagine that even those who are opposed to every inch of the Loyalty Program are worried when they realize that in the white primary fight in Georgia there were innumerable expensively printed gazettes and magazines favoring the white primary, and practically all of these carried fake names or no names.

Since the great minority groups, such as the National Association for the Advancement of Colored People, the CIO and the AFL, operating in most unfriendly areas, declared in favor of disclosure, I am still waiting for one example of a group which would have anything to fear by complete disclosure. To be sure, the shiftover from stealth to aboveboardness might cause some turmoil and discomfort, but I for my part am much more concerned with the discomfort of innocent people than I am with those who want to play an underground role. And with disclosure, in a very short time we will be able to defend more effectively *all* ideas in an open market place of thought.

Arthur E. Sutherland, Jr.:

THE INTERNAL SECURITY ACT OF 1950

FEDERAL legislation applicable to Communists and their organizations was quite abundant when the Internal Security Act of 1950 was passed. Treason and advocacy of the overthrow of the Government by force and violence were crimes. Agents of foreign governments were already required to register with the Attorney General and to label their propaganda. Any organization aiming at the forcible overthrow of the Government was required to register with the Attorney General, giving the names and addresses of officers and contributors of funds, with heavy penalties for failure to comply. Espionage and sabotage were crimes. Undermining the morale of the armed forces was penalized.

The United States already had considerable statutory protection against the immigration and sojourn within the country of subversive aliens. Such persons could not lawfully enter; if they nevertheless came in, they were deportable. Persons who believed in forceful overthrow of the Government could not be naturalized. Where they had obtained naturalization by fraudulent representations of their attachment to the United States, their naturalization could be cancelled. A statute in force since 1939 undertakes to protect the integrity of the Government by forbidding membership in Communist or like organizations to federal employees. The President's Loyalty Order reinforced this policy. Denial of passports, of tax advantages, and other minor sanctions expressed the intention of the Government to resist the activities of objectionable groups.

Despite the presence on the books of this rather considerable body of legislation, a mounting resentment throughout the United States against Communists and all their works has continued to manifest itself in legislation, both in municipalities and in states, and in pressure on Congress for new laws. The result was the passage on September 23 over the President's veto of the Internal Security Act of 1950. The new Act principally treats of four subjects. The first three of these are dealt with in Title I; it provides for the registration of "Communist organizations"; for the strengthening of the espionage laws; and for the amendment of the laws concerning immigration and naturalization. The fourth is found in Title II; it contains arrangements for the detention, in national emergencies, of potential spies and saboteurs.

The statute classifies those "Communist organizations" required to register as "Communist-action" and "Communist-front." A "Communist-action organization" is one which:

(i) is substantially directed, dominated, or controlled by the foreign government or foreign organization controlling the world Communist movement . . . and (ii) operates primarily to advance the objectives of such world Communist movements. . . .

From the *Harvard Law Review*, Vol. 64, No. 3 (January, 1951). Used by permission.

A "Communist-front" organization is one which:

(A) is substantially directed, dominated, or controlled by a Communist-action organization, and (B) is primarily operated for the purpose of giving aid and support to a Communist-action organization, a Communist foreign government, or the world Communist movement. . . .

"Front" organizations must register with the Attorney General, giving a list of officers and contributors of funds. "Action" organizations must give all the information required of front organizations, and, in addition, must list all their members. Their registers are to be open to public inspection. If an organization fails to register, the Attorney General petitions a Subversive Activities Control Board of five members for an order of enforcement. This Board, on petition of the Attorney General, is empowered to determine whether or not organizations which have failed to register are Communist-action,[1] or Communist-front and

to determine whether or not a person is a member of a Communist-action organization. The Board determines disputed questions after a hearing where the parties are entitled to appear with counsel.

Any party may obtain review of the Board's decision in the Court of Appeals for the District of Columbia, and the findings of the Board as to the facts, if supported by the preponderance of the evidence, are conclusive. Certiorari may be sought in the Supreme Court. When an order becomes final, it is enforceable by fines and imprisonment, and thereafter, radio broadcasts and mail must carry identification showing origin with a Communist organization; members are ineligible for nonelective federal employment; and members of action organizations may not work on defense contracts in private industry. Various other restrictions are imposed.

In the midst of the registration provisions, though without direct relation to them, occurs a section creating new crimes. Section 4(a) makes it unlawful knowingly to conspire to do any act, other than proposing a constitutional

---

[1] Internal Security Act § 13(e) provides:

In determining whether any organization is a "Communist-action organization," the Board shall take into consideration —
   (1) the extent to which its policies are formulated and carried out and its activities performed, pursuant to directives or to effectuate the policies of the foreign government or foreign organization in which is vested, or under the domination or control of which is exercised, the direction and control of the world Communist movement referred to in section 2 of this title; and
   (2) the extent to which its views and policies do not deviate from those of such foreign government or foreign organization; and
   (3) the extent to which it receives financial or other aid, directly or indirectly, from or at the direction of such foreign government or foreign organization; and
   (4) the extent to which it sends members or representatives to any foreign country for instruction or training in the principles, policies, strategy, or tactics of such world Communist movement; and

   (5) the extent to which it reports to such foreign government or foreign organization or to its representatives; and
   (6) the extent to which its principal leaders or a substantial number of its members are subject to or recognize the disciplinary power of such foreign government or foreign organization or its representatives; and
   (7) the extent to which, for the purpose of concealing foreign direction, domination, or control, or of expediting or promoting its objectives, (i) it fails to disclose, or resists efforts to obtain information as to, its membership (by keeping membership lists in code, by instructing members to refuse to acknowledge membership, or by any other method); (ii) its members refuse to acknowledge membership therein; (iii) it fails to disclose, or resists efforts to obtain information as to, records other than membership lists; (iv) its meetings are secret; and (v) it otherwise operates on a secret basis; . . .

amendment, "which would substantially contribute to the establishment within the United States of a totalitarian dictatorship" controlled from abroad. Other subsections of Section 4 provide new penalties for the unauthorized disclosure of classified information.

The second part of Title I incorporates a number of the suggestions of federal intelligence agencies for strengthening anti-espionage penalties. Prior espionage legislation is broadened to protect laboratories, to prohibit communication of defense information and to require government employees to report the loss of secret documents. The period of limitations for espionage crimes is lengthened to ten years. Persons who have received foreign training in espionage are required to register with the Attorney General, and a war measure is revived which punishes persons who violate regulations promulgated by the Secretary of Defense for the protection of military establishments.

The third portion of Title I drastically amends the immigration and naturalization laws. The Attorney General's discretion is broadened with respect to destinations to which he can deport aliens, and registered aliens are required to report changes of address. Persons who advocate the doctrines of world Communism and members of the Communist-action organizations which are required to register, are not eligible for naturalization, and citizens who join such organizations within five years after being naturalized may have their naturalization cancelled. The most striking provision of this part excludes from the United States any alien who at any time in his life was a member of or affiliated with any totalitarian party, or any of its subdivisions, or any organization registerable under the Act.

Title II provides for the detention, if the President proclaims "an internal security emergency," of those persons found by the Detention Review Board to be likely spies or saboteurs. Such an emergency occurs only when the United States or its possessions is invaded, or when the Congress declares war, or when there occurs within the United States an insurrection in aid of a foreign enemy. Persons objecting to detention have available an elaborate system of review by the Board and the federal courts.[2]

President Truman on September 22, 1950, returned this bill without his approval. His veto message stated that the departments of Defense, State, Justice and the Central Intelligence Agency had all advised him that the measure would seriously damage their operations, and had expressed the hope that it would not become law. He listed seven specific objections. It would:

2 After the proclamation of an emergency, detainable persons can be apprehended upon the issuance of warrants by the Attorney General. *Id.* § 104(a). Within 48 hours after being apprehended, the detainee has a preliminary hearing where he is advised of his rights and of the grounds for his detention; he may be represented by counsel and introduce evidence. *Id.* § 104(d). The hearing officer may order the detainee discharged and the Attorney General has no appeal from such an order. *Ibid.* However, if the hearing examiner sees probable cause for holding the detainee and issues a detention order, the detainee may appeal to the Detention Review Board. *Id.* § 109(a). The nine man board, or a three man division thereof, reviews the hearing examiner's finding, subject to provisions of the Administrative Procedure Act. *Id.* §§ 110, 111(g). The Board may confirm, modify, or revoke the detention order, and may indemnify the detainee for loss of income. *Id.* § 110. A detainee, aggrieved by a Board order, is entitled to judicial review in a court of appeals; the Attorney General is entitled to judicial review of indemnity orders but not of Board orders revoking or modifying detention orders. *Id.* § 111(a)–(c). Certiorari to the Supreme Court lies for reviewable orders. *Id.* § 111(d). Criminal provisions impose fine and imprisonment upon detainees who escape and on their accomplices. *Id.* §§ 112, 113. See also p. 410 *infra*.

(1) require publication of a list of defense installations;

(2) require the Department of Justice and FBI to waste time and energy attempting to enforce unworkable registration provisions;

(3) deprive us of the assistance of many aliens in intelligence matters;

(4) antagonize friendly governments;

(5) put the Government of the United States in the thought-control business;

(6) facilitate naturalization of subversive aliens;

(7) give government officials vast powers to harass all citizens in the exercise of their right of free speech.

The President went on to develop his objections to the bill at greater length, saying that the requirement for registration of Communist-front organizations could be the greatest danger to freedom of speech, press and assembly since the Alien and Sedition Laws of 1798.

The Congress passed the measure over his veto, in the House on September 22 and in the Senate on September 23. Only 48 votes were cast to sustain the veto in the House, against 286 to override, with 95 not voting. In the Senate 10 voted to sustain the veto, with 57 to override, and 29 not voting.

The new legislation is a mosaic of several proposals, some of which have been before the Congress for several years. The detention, the espionage-sabotage, and certain deportation provisions originated in whole or in part with proposals made by the executive branch or by Senators friendly to it. S. 4061, introduced by Senator Lehman, was described as the "administration internal security bill." This bill recited a number of statutes then in force which provided means of suppressing Communist activity, men-

tioned the President's loyalty program as established under the authority of "other provisions of law" and recommended that "such statutes should be vigorously enforced so as to minimize the present danger to the national security resulting from activities of associations and individuals aiding and supporting the world Communist movement." The bill contained proposals to strengthen existing espionage laws, and its principal provisions appear in the Internal Security Act of 1950 as Sections 18–21. This administration bill also contributed Section 23 of the final legislation which strengthens the hand of the Attorney General in deportation matters.

On September 6, 1950, Senator Kilgore introduced S. 4130, a new "Internal Security Act of 1950," repeating the provisions of the administration bill, and adding Title II, which its sponsors termed "The Emergency Detention Act of 1950," and which became Title II of the legislation as finally enacted. The President, in his veto message, objected to these detention provisions because they failed to provide for suspension of the writ of habeas corpus and so might prove unenforceable; and because persons other than those covered by the Act might be more important to detain.

Section 22 of the final legislation, excluding from the United States aliens who in the past have belonged to any form of totalitarian party or its subdivisions, or who engage in totalitarian activity, originated in a bill introduced by Senator McCarran in 1949 and passed by the Senate on August 9, 1950. Sections 25–30, amending the Nationality Act of 1940 to prohibit the naturalization of Communists, and to provide drastic denaturalization regulations, stem from Senator McCarran's S. 3455, introduced in April, 1950.

The registration sections, the most controversial part of the Internal Security Act of 1950, derive from the Mundt-Nixon bill, which was passed by the House of Representatives of the 80th Congress but then allowed to die in the Senate Committee on the Judiciary. Its provisions were vigorously opposed by the President in his veto message, met the most cutting opposition on the floor of the Senate from the group who had sponsored other parts of the legislation, and have been much criticized by many thoughtful commentators. That part of the registration provisions which included nondeviation from Communist-action policies as a criterion of identifying a Communist-front organization was singled out for criticism by the President in his veto message. It is probably the most disputed feature of the entire new statute.

Senator Karl Mundt:

THE CASE FOR THE McCARRAN ACT

MR. President, I desire now to discuss some of the criticisms made of the bill[1] yesterday, because they pretty well run the whole gamut of available criticisms. They can be found in various forms by reading the Daily Worker, by listening to the left-wing commentators on the air, by reading the left-wing columnists in newspapers, and by reading the criticisms of honest, decent, legitimate Americans who have doubts about the bill.

The junior Senator from New York (Mr. Lehman) yesterday engaged in the well-known parliamentary practice of throwing everything at the bill, hoping that something would stick. So he used everything from the outright Communist arguments appearing in the Communist press to the arguments presented by persons who have legitimate doubts and

[1] The "Mundt-Ferguson Bill," S. 2311.

fears and who represent a good political viewpoint. . . .

The Senator from New York began by saying:

We already have on the statute books more than 20 laws to control and penalize subversive activities such as espionage, sabotage, and failure to register as a foreign agent.

I think that is a statement of fact. I know it is certainly a statement of fact that in spite of those laws, Alger Hiss was able to work his way into the State Department and to carry on, through a series of years, an espionage campaign, the ramifications of which we have not yet discovered or terminated. No one knows, as yet, how much of the nasty work done by Alger Hiss and his associates at Yalta is being paid for by the blood of American boys in Korea. Whatever he has con-

Extracts from speech in U. S. Senate, *Congressional Record,* Vol. 96, 14415–14436 (No. 177, September 6, 1950).

tributed to the chaos and confusion which confront us was done in spite of the 20 laws referred to by the Senator from New York. Hiss was finally brought to book not because of any of those laws, but because he lied before a Federal grand jury about his participation in the espionage racket.

Julian Wadleigh is running around Washington loose today, after having admitted that more than 500 different times he smuggled State Department documents out of that department and delivered them to Communists. "Admitted" is too mild a term. He boasted about it, and he sold his syndicated confessions to the American press for $5,000. He is 100 percent scot-free. If we follow the counsel of the junior Senator from New York, such espionage agents are going to continue to be 100 percent scot-free, in spite of the 20 laws on the books. There can be no question about that.

We can enumerate cases of spies who have been operating recently, and who have been operating without being caught because of any of these laws. We can enumerate a whole series of cases of that kind.

Further on in the argument of the junior Senator from New York he said:

What dyed-in-the-wool Communist will run to the nearest registration office to list himself as such and expose himself to the penalties contained in the Mundt-Ferguson bill?

We may hear that argument repeated, but I hope we shall not. Let us analyze that argument and see of what kind of puerile stuff it is made. Why pass a law, he says, when a Communist will not give himself up? Can we not apply that argument to a murderer as well? Murderers do not have the habit of delivering themselves to courts of law. Why have a law against white slavery? Do those who commit that crime give themselves up? Why have laws against counterfeiting? Do counterfeiters give themselves up? Do kidnapers give themselves up? If we are going to follow in this country the theory that because we pass laws people are going to form in line and deliver themselves into the hands of justice, we had better fold up and go home and let more sturdy souls take our places in this body.

That is the essence of the argument of the Senator from New York. He asks, "Who is going to list himself and expose himself to the penalties of the law?" The answer is, if they do not do it they will be treated just as is any other person who does not obey the law in connection with counterfeiting or any other Federal legislation. If he is caught, he goes to jail; and such persons usually go to jail. That is what happens to any law violator. We cannot operate on the theory that we should not pass a law because a criminal is not going voluntarily to deliver himself into the hands of the law. . . .

The Senator from New York would compare our proposed legislation with the alien and sedition laws. There is absolutely no relationship and no resemblance between the two. Our proposed legislation does not provide any of the curtailments involved in the alien and sedition laws, as a reading of the bill will disclose, if it is read in the light of day. . . .

Mr. President, I wish to associate myself with one statement which the junior Senator from New York made yesterday. . . . [He] said that Al Smith denounced the expulsion of the Socialists from the New York Legislature in these words:

Our faith in American democracy is confirmed not only by its results but by its methods and organs of free expression. They are the safeguards against revolution. To discard the methods of representative government leads to the misdeeds of the very extremists we denounce — and serves to increase the number of the enemies of orderly free government.

Mr. President, I associate myself with every syllable, word, and phrase of that statement. I submit that the so-called Mundt-Ferguson bill would follow that mandate precisely. Under our proposed legislation Communists could elect their officials and send them to Congress, if they could get the votes. We would permit Communists to hold elective office, to have access to the ballot, to run for President, Vice President, or Congress. Furthermore, if the laws of their States permitted, they could run for any local offices, exactly as Al Smith suggested. Let me repeat what Al Smith said:

> To destroy the methods of representative government leads to the misdeeds of the very extremists we denounce.

The next complaint lodged against the Mundt-Ferguson bill is this: The Senator from New York says that he is opposed to the provision of the bill which makes Communist organizations label the printed material they send through the mail, and he calls attention to it because, he says, the contents of the literature or letters will be immaterial. In other words, I dare say he proposes setting up a censorship: I presume he proposes establishing another kind of Gestapo activity.

I am not concerned about what the Communists send through the mail provided they label it so that people will know where it comes from. I do not want anybody snooping around and saying that Communists or Democrats or Re-

publicans can send things through the mails anonymously if a censor does not disapprove the contents. I want the Communists to do what Republicans and Democrats have to do in campaign time, under the law, put the label of the party on anything they print and circulate, and let them be answerable for it. I am not concerned with censoring the contents. I do not care whether it is an invitation to a tea party or a call to revolt. Let it be identified by the label of the party. Let the Communists assume responsibility for their propaganda.

I want the junior Senator from New York or someone else sponsoring the milk toast amendment proposed as the administration's substitute to tell me why they want to continue to give a cyclone cellar of concealment to Communists when we have found it necessary to deny it to Republicans and Democrats. I do not believe in anonymous campaigns, anonymous letters, and anonymous attacks.

I wholeheartedly subscribe to the theory that a candidate for public office should sign the literature that goes through the mail in his behalf, or have it attributable to a definite and responsible source. I am not one who would say, "That is a good rule for Republicans and Democrats, but because we might lose a few left-wing votes in the city precincts we do not want to apply it to the Communists." This particular Senator can be counted out when it comes to that kind of appeasement of the Communists.

Let me read the next statement of the junior Senator from New York:

> No individual writing to wife, husband, broker, lawyer, or doctor will be sure that the communication will not be read and abstracted by some agent in pursuit of evidence that this letter was one of those mailed by

a Communist or Communist-front organization.

What a perversion of the contents of the bill! Whom is that designed to deceive? Certainly no Member of the Senate, because most Members of the Senate are going to read the bill before they act upon it. It is provided specifically in the bill that the provision referred to deals only with printed material which is designed to be circulated and disseminated among two or more people. No private letter, individually addressed, could conceivably come under that kind of definition, and certainly the Senator must know it. That is why I say we cannot afford to confuse ourselves by irresponsible statements made about proposed legislation so vital to the safety of America in time of war as is this kind of Communist-control legislation.

Mr. President, now I come to an argument of the Senator from New York which has to be answered, and it is probably as strained an interpretation of the bill as I have ever heard anywhere. The last time I heard it was when it was delivered on the floor of the House of Representatives by a Representative from the city of New York, Representative VITO MARCANTONIO. When I was working on a similar bill about 3 years ago I listened to the same kind of talk in the House. I listened to it again yesterday. I answered it then, and I shall answer it now, and I shall answer it at any other time when anyone tries to place that kind of shotgun interpretation upon legislation which has been sustained, as this has, by the outstanding legal talent in America, in addition to the Committee on the Judiciary, as I have said; including representative committees of the American Bar Association, several State bar associations, the firm of John W.

Davis & Co., the law faculty of the University of Virginia, and many others.

I shall now quote from page 14372 of the Record of yesterday, September 5. On that page appears a colloquy between the Senator from New York (Mr. Lehman) and the Senator from Illinois (Mr. Douglas) in the course of which the Senator from New York said:

Under the terms of the Mundt-Ferguson and McCarran bills, good American organizations — labor unions, church groups, and others — could be charged on this basis with being Communist fronts.

Then he points out the criteria, or little bits or parts of the criteria, involved to indicate how he thinks that there could be indicted as Communist-front organizations a whole series of organizations, such as church groups, CARE, labor unions — anybody who favors the Brannan plan, the FEPC, or socialized medicine. Then says the Senator from New York:

But the really significant point lies in the fact that the bill leaves it entirely to the discretion of the Subversive Activities Control Board —

Which is erroneous. The bill leaves it in the first place to the control of the Attorney General.

In the second instance, decisions based on hearings held by the Subversive Activities Control Board can be taken to the appellate courts. So that at best it can be said that the Senator was only 33⅓ percent accurate in that statement.

Then he goes on to state how labor, how the United Auto Workers of America, for example, were to be brought under the terms of the bill. He spent a considerable amount of time alleging that they can be brought under the terms of the measure. I think that allegation should be answered because certainly it is a fair question for discussion whether or not the bill is designed to bring under its provisions labor organizations, farm organizations, and other perfectly legitimate organizations. I think the best answer is to read the bill. I think we could have saved ourselves a great deal of time yesterday and today if it had been a sort of standard practice by those discussing the measure to indulge in at least a cursory, perfunctory reading of the bill before the pontification begins. On page 7 we find this language:

The term "Communist-controlled organization" means any organization in the United States which (a) is substantially dominated or controlled by the foreign government or foreign governmental or political organization controlling the world Communist movement referred to in section 2.

That knocks into the ashcan two columns of the Senator's argument when he tries to make us believe that we are going to become involved in totalitarian government controls such as those in China, Yugoslavia, and so forth. The Senator knows and other Senators know and I know where communism is controlled. It is controlled in Moscow.

The bill points out exactly the kind of Communist-controlled organization it refers to. It says:

Which is substantially dominated or controlled by the foreign government or foreign governmental or political organization controlling the world Communist movement referred to in section 2, and (b) operates primarily to advance the objectives of such world Communist movement, as set forth in section 2 of this act.

Obviously no one could bring within that kind of definition any labor union or any church group or the packages sent out by CARE. Labor and farm organizations, churches and relief organizations are of course not even remotely affected by the Mundt-Ferguson provisions.

So let us look at the other part of Communist-front organization. What is a Communist-front organization?

The term "Communist-front organization" means any organization in the United States (other than a Communist-controlled organization) . . .

Which is the one I have just defined — which (a) is under the control of a Communist-controlled organization.

It would be necessary to bring the UAWA under the provisions of the bill to show that the Union of Auto Workers is under the control of the Communist Party. If that is true they would have to register. The Senator from New York denies it is true that the UAWA is under such control. I deny it is true. I do not know anyone who alleges it is true. But only if, when, and as it is true that it is under the control of the Communist Party, does any organization become a Communist-front organization, such as the American Youth for Democracy, the League for Peace and Democracy, and organizations of that nature. There is just not any use trying to scare a lot of innocent people by saying, "You are going to have to register as a Communist-front organization before you can send a CARE package to a family living in Poland." I think the times are a little bit too serious for that kind of misrepresentation of legislation so vital to our security as this is. That is why I have taken the time to correct the statements that have been made, far from the point though they were.

What other kind of Communist-front organization could there be? It either has to be controlled by the Communists or else "(b) is primarily operated for the purpose of giving aid and support to a Communist-controlled organization, a Communist foreign government, or the World Communist Movement referred to in section 2."

Its primary, fundamental, basic purpose must be to support the Communist Government in Russia, or to support world communism, or to support the foreign Communist organizations in the United States. It is utterly and absurdly ridiculous to assume it applies to labor unions. I inserted in the Record a letter about two weeks ago from Louis Waldman in which he pointed out that of the most absurd representation respecting the bill is the one in which it is suggested that it referred to labor unions, to farm organizations, to church groups. It applies only to what it says it applies to, nothing more and nothing less.

Mr. President . . .

Said the Senator from New York — and Members of the Senate, in the Mundt-Ferguson and McCarran bills, we have legislation which permits thought policing.

Again I offer to quote as against that the provisions of the bill on the floor of the Senate. If the junior Senator from New York or any other Senator can quote a paragraph, a syllable, or a sentence anywhere in the bill which provides for thought policing, I challenge him to do it. Quite the contrary is true, as I propose to show later. We give to the Communists every single legitimate political privilege and freedom to function now enjoyed by the Democratic and Republican Parties of the United States. I submit to the Senate in all sincerity, in the middle of a war we should not have to listen to misrepresentations of that kind which are refutable simply by reading

the bill. There is no thought policing in the bill. There is no censorship provided in it. In fact, we would compel Communists to register publications without censoring. . . .

Mr. President, what does the bill provide? First of all, it is built, as I have said before, on a simple, three-pronged formula. We propose to identify Communists, we propose to disclose communism, and we propose to curtail certain Communist activities.

We propose to move against communism to the minimum degree which is compatible with the safety of our American Republic.

We propose to move against Communists by act of law, not by executive fiat or decree.

We propose to safeguard our Government against communism within the constitutional provision of our charter of freedom, the Constitution of the United States.

The first requirement is that Communists register. I have already mentioned that. Why not require Communists to register, Mr. President? Republicans register and Democrats register in most of the States of the Union, even to vote in the primaries. Republicans and Democrats register in every State of the Union before they can go to a political convention and participate in the selection of nominees or candidates. Today, registered Democrats are meeting in one town in New York and registered Republicans are meeting in another town in New York to select gubernatorial and senatorial candidates. Does that mean that any foot-loose Republicans should go to the Democratic convention or that any foot-loose Democrats should go to the Republican convention and should attempt to mess it up by trying to participate in the selection of their candidates? No one advocates such a thing. However, there are those who say that Communists should not have to register.

Mr. President, the principle of registration has been established in this country down through the years. We have on the statute books laws requiring the registration of stocks and other securities; and I am in favor of it, and I think it is a good thing. We have on the statute books laws requiring good, patriotic Americans to register as lobbyists if they appear before a congressional committee; and I am in favor of it, and I think it is a good thing. It does not deny anyone the right to function freely, but it simply lets others know who they are and whom they represent.

However, there are those who say it is all right to say to the head of a labor union or to the representative of a farmers' group or farm organization, "You must register as a lobbyist before you can come to Washington," but who do not think those who represent Joe Stalin should be required to register. Mr. President, Senators can count me out on that kind of appeasement, for I am against it.

Registration is a reasonable device applied today to good Americans. We simply want to apply it also to bad and disloyal Americans. Let those who want to defend special privileges for disloyal Americans defend them, but not on the ground that registration is something novel or something new or something unprecedented. In these halls registration is an established principle of disclosure, which has been used over and over and over again.

Mr. President, in addition to requiring Communists to register, the bill requires Communists to identify their activities. I have mentioned that, too. The bill also requires Communists to identify their fronts.

When the national Democratic organization organizes a Young Democrats League they have to identify it as such. Why not, Mr. President? When the national Republican organization organizes a Republican woman's organization they have to identify it as such. Why not, Mr. President? Who are ashamed of their convictions and their beliefs except the traitors in our midst and the espionage agents and those who want to do dirty work in the darkness of the night? Why should not Communists be required to identify themselves, just as Democrats and Republicans are required to do? Why does not someone answer that question?

Let some of the sponsors of the fourth version of the administration's substitute, which was submitted about ten minutes ago by the Senator from West Virginia (Mr. Kilgore), for himself and other Senators, answer that question. Believe me, Mr. President, they are changing their versions rather rapidly. Why do not they say why they do not want Communists to register and to identify themselves? Why do not they say why they do not want Communist revenue and Communist propaganda and membership identified? They owe that to the boys who are fighting and dying in Korea.

Mr. President, let me say a few words about what the bill does not do. What is it that the Communists claim it does that it does not do? What is it that the synthetic liberals and pseudo-progressives claim it does that it does not do? What is it that all the slimy literature sent out by the so-called National Committee To Defeat the Mundt Bill says it does which it does not do?

It does not deny free speech. If it did

that, it would be a police-state bill. I have offered to eat every bill introduced in the Senate if in any way it can be found that this bill curtails thought or speech.

It does not in any way deny anyone free speech, no matter how traitorous he may be. It does not deny freedom of assembly to anyone. The Communists can still have their meetings in New York, at the home headquarters of the Daily Worker. They can still operate their Jefferson School in Chicago. They can still have their meetings in Madison Square and their front organizations to keep the rest of them operating.

The bill does not deny freedom of movement or freedom of the mails, or freedom of publication to anyone. It simply says to the Communists as it says to the editors of the Saturday Evening Post, "You have got to identify with the imprimatur of ownership all publications sent through the mails; you must show who it is who is responsible." It stops that anonymous means of deception in which Communists specialize. It makes them stand responsible for the stuff they spew out through the mails and over the broadcasting stations.

It does not deny any freedom of speech, freedom of assembly, freedom of movement, freedom of the mails, or any freedom of thought. That is not in the bill; it cannot be found in the bill, and if it is claimed it is there, from now on kindly spell out the chapter and the section in which it is found. Why try to confuse the people?

It does not deny a Communist the use of the ballot. . . .

I believe in the free and open ballot. If 51 percent or 52 percent of the people in America want to elect Communist Members of Congress, or even elect a Communist President, let them vote for them openly. If they do, I will take the first ship to Scandinavia, or some place like that. However, I am in favor of giving them the right to the ballot. . . .

Finally, this bill does not deny — and I want Senators to note that fact particularly, because the bill is a disappointment to some people — a single open — and let us note the word "open" — political propaganda activity in which the Communist Party is now engaged. Not one. There is nothing of a propaganda or political nature which the Communist Party of America now does which it would not be able to do under the proposed legislation, except that they would have to do it in the open.

Why do they whine so much in the Daily Worker? Why do they snivel and whine and moan about this legislation? Because they know that if they have to operate in the open Americans will repel and reject their godless doctrine. Their only chance to win in America is in the dark, secretly, and by stealth. We strip the mantle of secrecy from Communists and force them out into the open precisely as long advocated by J. Edgar Hoover of the FBI.

I say to the weeping sob sisters, who insist that the bill goes too far, that the bill does not deny Communists freedom of speech, freedom of the press, freedom of the mails, freedom of movement, or freedom of assembly. It does not deny Communists the right to engage in every political propaganda activity in which they are now engaged. It simply forces them to do those things in the open, exactly as we require the Democratic and Republican Parties to act in the open.

Mr. MARTIN. Does not the Senator feel that we in America need something to arouse the American people as to just what the American way of life stands for?

MR. MUNDT. I think that unless they can be so aroused they are going to lose their freedom. . . .

To me it is an appalling fact — and I say this as a former educator — that after 150 years of what has become admittedly the best educational system in the world, we do not have a textbook in this country in our high schools and colleges at this late hour which genuinely tells the story of American freedom and independence. There is a book on communism; there is a book on nazism; there is a book on Leninism; but none as an adequate and usable textbook on that great opportunity State made possible by our formula of freedom.

MR. MARTIN. As the distinguished Senator well knows, there is a book on practically every philosophy of govern-ment in the world except the American philosophy of government, which is the greatest form of government that has ever been created.

MR. MUNDT. Even the British Social-ists, who have been in power for less than six years, have a book relating what that government is, written by John Strachey, that curious member of the British Cabi-net who was formerly a Communist and is now a Socialist. He wrote a textbook for the Socialists of Great Britain called How Socialism Works. There is not in this country a realization on the part of a great many individuals that, if we are to remain free, we must do more than simply talk about it and grumble about taxes. We shall have to do something to protect the basic ingredients from which freedom is created.

President Harry S. Truman:

THE INTERNAL SECURITY ACT:
Veto Message

TO the House of Representatives: I return herewith, without my ap-proval, H. R. 9490, the proposed "Inter-nal Security Act of 1950."

I am taking this action only after the most serious study and reflection and after consultation with the security and intelligence agencies of the Government. The Department of Justice, the Depart-ment of Defense, the Central Intelligence Agency, and the Department of State have all advised me that the bill would seriously damage the security and intelli-gence operations for which they are re-sponsible. They have strongly expressed the hope that the bill would not become law.

This is an omnibus bill containing many different legislative proposals with only one thing in common: they are all

Delivered to the House of Representatives, Washington, D. C., September 22, 1950. [Only those passages of the message are reproduced which relate to the so-called Mundt-Ferguson sections of the McCarran Act. Ed.]

represented to be "anticommunist." But when the many complicated pieces of the bill are analyzed in detail, a startling result appears.

H. R. 9490 would not hurt the communists. Instead, it would help them.

It has been claimed over and over again that this is an "anticommunist" bill — a "communist control" bill. But in actual operation the bill would have results exactly the opposite of those intended.

It would actually weaken our existing internal security measures and would seriously hamper the Federal Bureau of Investigation and our other security agencies.

It would help the communists in their efforts to create dissension and confusion within our borders.

It would help the communist propagandists throughout the world who are trying to undermine freedom by discrediting as hypocrisy the efforts of the United States on behalf of freedom.

Specifically, some of the principal objections to the bill are as follows:

1. It would aid potential enemies by requiring the publication of a complete list of vital defense plants, laboratories, and other installations.

2. It would require the Department of Justice and its Federal Bureau of Investigation to waste immense amounts of time and energy attempting to carry out its unworkable registration provisions.

3. It would deprive us of the great assistance of many aliens in intelligence matters.

4. It would antagonize friendly governments.

5. It would put the Government of the United States in the thought-control business.

6. It would make it easier for subversive aliens to become naturalized as United States citizens.

7. It would give Government officials vast powers to harass all of our citizens in the exercise of their right of free speech.

Legislation with these consequences is not necessary to meet the real dangers which communism presents to our free society. Those dangers are serious and must be met. But this bill would hinder us, not help us, in meeting them. Fortunately, we already have on the books strong laws which give us most of the protection we need from the real dangers of treason, espionage, sabotage, and actions looking to the overthrow of our Government by force and violence. Most of the provisions of this bill have no relation to these real dangers.

One provision alone of this bill is enough to demonstrate how far it misses the real target. Section 5 would require the Secretary of Defense to "proclaim" and "have published in the Federal Register" a public catalogue of defense plants, laboratories, and all other facilities vital to our national defense — no matter how secret. I cannot imagine any document a hostile foreign government would desire more. Spies and saboteurs would willingly spend years of effort seeking to find out the information that this bill would require the Government to hand them on a silver platter. There are many provisions of this bill which impel me to return it without my approval, but this one would be enough by itself. It is inconceivable to me that a majority of the Congress could expect the Commander in Chief of the Armed Forces of the United States to approve such a flagrant violation of proper security safeguards.

This is only one example of many provisions in the bill which would in actual practice work to the detriment of our national security.

I know that the Congress had no intention of achieving such results when it passed this bill. I know that the vast majority of the Members of Congress who voted for the bill sincerely intended to strike a blow at the Communists.

It is true that certain provisions of this bill would improve the laws protecting us against espionage and sabotage. But these provisions are greatly outweighed by others which would actually impair our security.

I repeat, the net results of this bill would be to help the Communists, not to hurt them.

I therefore most earnestly request the Congress to reconsider its action. I am confident that on more careful analysis most Members of Congress will recognize that this bill is contrary to the best interests of our country at this critical time.

H. R. 9490 is made up of a number of different parts. In summary, their purposes and probable effects may be described as follows:

Sections 1 through 17 are designed for two purposes. First, they are intended to force Communist organizations to register and to divulge certain information about themselves — information on their officers, their finances, and, in some cases, their membership. These provisions would in practice be ineffective and would result in obtaining no information about Communists that the FBI and our other security agencies do not already have. But in trying to enforce these sections, we would have to spend a great deal of time, effort, and money — all to no good purpose.

Second, these provisions are intended to impose various penalties on Communists and others covered by the terms of the bill. So far as Communists are concerned, all these penalties which can be

practicably enforced are already in effect under existing laws and procedures. But the language of the bill is so broad and vague that it might well result in penalizing the legitimate activities of people who are not Communists at all, but loyal citizens.

Thus the net result of these sections of the bill would be: no serious damage to the Communists, much damage to the rest of us. Only the Communist movement would gain from such an outcome. . . .

Because I feel so strongly that this legislation would be a terrible mistake, I want to discuss more fully its worse features — sections 1 through 17, and sections 22 and 25.

Most of the first 17 sections of H. R. 9490 are concerned with requiring registration and annual reports, by what the bill calls Communist-action organizations and Communist-front organizations, of names of officers, sources and uses of funds, and in the case of Communist-action organizations, names of members.

The idea of requiring Communist organizations to divulge information about themselves is a simple and attractive one. But it is about as practical as requiring thieves to register with the sheriff. Obviously, no such organization as the Communist Party is likely to register voluntarily.

Under the provisions of the bill, if an organization which the Attorney General believes should register does not do so, he must request a five-man Subversive Activities Control Board to order the organization to register. The Attorney General would have to produce proof that the organization in question was in fact a Communist-action or a Communist-front organization. To do this he would have to offer evidence relating to every aspect of the organization's activities. The organization could present opposing evidence. Prolonged hearings would be required to allow both sides to present proof and to cross-examine opposing witnesses.

To estimate the duration of such a proceeding involving the Communist Party, we need only recall that on much narrower issues the trial of the 11 Communist leaders under the Smith Act consumed 9 months. In a hearing under this bill, the difficulties of proof would be much greater and would take a much longer time.

The bill lists a number of criteria for the Board to consider in deciding whether or not an organization is a Communist-action or Communist-front organization. Many of these deal with the attitudes or states of mind of the organization's leaders. It is frequently difficult in legal proceedings to establish whether or not a man has committed an overt act, such as theft or perjury. But under this bill, the Attorney General would have to attempt the immensely more difficult task of producing concrete legal evidence that men have particular ideas or opinions. This would inevitably require the disclosure of many of the FBI's confidential sources of information and thus would damage our national security.

If, eventually, the Attorney General should overcome these difficulties and get a favorable decision from the Board, the Board's decision could be appealed to the courts. The courts would review any questions of law involved, and whether the Board's findings of fact were supported by the preponderance of the evidence.

All these proceedings would require great effort and much time. It is almost certain that from 2 to 4 years would elapse between the Attorney General's decision to go before the Board with a

case, and the final disposition of the matter by the courts.

And when all this time and effort had been spent, it is still most likely that no organization would actually register.

The simple fact is that when the courts at long last found that a particular organization was required to register, all the leaders of the organization would have to do to frustrate the law would be to dissolve the organization and establish a new one with a different name and a new roster of nominal officers. The Communist Party has done this again and again in countries throughout the world. And nothing could be done about it except to begin all over again the long dreary process of investigative, administrative, and judicial proceedings to require registration.

Thus the net result of the registration provision of this bill would probably be an endless chasing of one organization after another, with the Communists always able to frustrate the law enforcement agencies and prevent any final result from being achieved. It could only result in wasting the energies of the Department of Justice and in destroying the sources of information of its FBI. To impose these fruitless burdens upon the FBI would divert it from its vital security duties and thus give aid and comfort to the very Communists whom the bill is supposed to control.

Unfortunately, these provisions are not merely ineffective and unworkable. They represent a clear and present danger to our institutions.

Insofar as the bill would require registration by the Communist Party itself, it does not endanger our traditional liberties. However, the application of the registration requirements to so-called Communist-front organizations can be the greatest danger to freedom of speech, press, and assembly, since the Alien and Sedition Laws of 1798. This danger arises out of the criteria or standards to be applied in determining whether an organization is a Communist-front organization.

There would be no serious problem if the bill required proof that an organization was controlled and financed by the Communist Party before it could be classified as a Communist-front organization. However, recognizing the difficulty of proving those matters, the bill would permit such a determination to be based solely upon the extent to which the positions taken or advanced by it from time to time on matters of policy do not deviate from those of the Communist movement.

This provision could easily be used to classify as a Communist-front organization any organization which is advocating a single policy or objective which is also being urged by the Communist Party or by a Communist foreign government. In fact, this may be the intended result, since the bill defines "organization" to include "a group of persons permanently or temporarily associated together for joint action on any subject or subjects." Thus, an organization which advocates low-cost housing for sincere humanitarian reasons might be classified as a Communist-front organization because the Communists regularly exploit slum conditions as one of their fifth-column techniques.

It is not enough to say that this probably would not be done. The mere fact that it could be done shows clearly how the bill would open a Pandora's box of opportunities for official condemnation of organizations and individuals for perfectly honest opinions which happen to be stated also by Communists.

The basic error of these sections is that they move in the direction of suppressing opinion and belief. This would be a very dangerous course to take, not because we have any sympathy for Communist opinions, but because any governmental stifling of the free expression of opinion is a long step toward totalitarianism.

There is no more fundamental axiom of American freedom than the familiar statement: In a free country, we punish men for the crimes they commit, but never for the opinions they have. And the reason this is so fundamental to freedom is not, as many suppose, that it protects the few unorthodox from suppression by the majority. To permit freedom of expression is primarily for the benefit of the majority because it protects criticism, and criticism leads to progress.

We can and we will prevent espionage, sabotage, or other actions endangering our national security. But we would betray our finest traditions if we attempted, as this bill would attempt, to curb the simple expression of opinion. This we should never do, no matter how distasteful the opinion may be to the vast majority of our people. The course proposed by this bill would delight the Communists, for it would make a mockery of the Bill of Rights and of our claims to stand for freedom in the world.

And what kind of effect would these provisions have on the normal expression of political views? Obviously, if this law were on the statute books, the part of prudence would be to avoid saying anything that might be construed by someone as not deviating sufficiently from the current Communist propaganda line. And since no one could be sure in advance what views were safe to express, the inevitable tendency would be to express no views on controversial subjects.

The result could only be to reduce the vigor and strength of our political life — an outcome that the Communists would happily welcome, but that free men should abhor.

We need not fear the expression of ideas — we do need to fear their suppression.

Our position in the vanguard of freedom rests largely on our demonstration that the free expression of opinion, coupled with government by popular consent, leads to national strength and human advancement. Let us not, in cowering and foolish fear, throw away the ideals which are the fundamental basis of our free society.

Not only are the registration provisions of this bill unworkable and dangerous, they are also grossly misleading in that all but one of the objectives which are claimed for them are already being accomplished by other and superior methods — and the one objective which is not now being accomplished would not in fact be accomplished under this bill either.

It is claimed that the bill would provide information about the Communist Party and its members. The fact is, the FBI already possesses very complete sources of information concerning the Communist movement in this country. If the FBI must disclose its sources of information in public hearings to require registration under this bill, its present sources of information, and its ability to acquire new information, will be largely destroyed.

It is claimed that this bill would deny income-tax exemption to Communist organizations. The fact is that the Bureau of Internal Revenue already denies income-tax exemption to such organizations.

It is claimed that this bill would deny passports to Communists. The fact is that the Government can and does deny passports to Communists under existing law.

It is claimed that this bill would prohibit the employment of Communists by the Federal Government. The fact is that the employment of Communists by the Federal Government is already prohibited and, at least in the executive branch, there is an effective program to see that they are not employed.

It is claimed that this bill would prohibit the employment of Communists in defense plants. The fact is that it would be years before this bill would have any effect of this nature — if it ever would. Fortunately, this objective is already being substantially achieved under the present procedures of the Department of Defense, and if the Congress would enact one of the provisions I have recommended — which it did not include in this bill — the situation would be entirely taken care of, promptly and effectively.

It is also claimed — and this is the one new objective of the registration provisions of this bill — that it would require Communist organizations to label all their publications and radio and television broadcasts as emanating from a Communist source. The fact is that this requirement, even if constitutional, could be easily and permanently evaded, simply by the continuous creation of new organizations to distribute Communist information.

Section 4 (a) of the bill, like its registration provisions, would be ineffective, would be subject to dangerous abuse, and would seek to accomplish an objective which is already better accomplished under existing law.

This provision would make unlawful any agreement to perform any act which would substantially contribute to the establishment within the United States of a foreign-controlled dictatorship. Of course, this provision would be unconstitutional if it infringed upon the fundamental right of the American people to establish for themselves by constitutional methods any form of government they choose. To avoid this, it is provided that this section shall not apply to the proposal of a constitutional amendment. If this language limits the prohibition of the section to the use of unlawful methods, then it adds nothing to the Smith Act, under which 11 Communist leaders have been convicted, and would be more difficult to enforce. Thus, it would accomplish nothing. Moreover, the bill does not even purport to define the phrase, unique in a criminal statute, "substantially contribute." A phrase so vague raises a serious constitutional question. . . .

Earlier this month, we launched a great Crusade for Freedom designed, in the words of General Eisenhower, to fight the big lie with the big truth. I can think of no better way to make a mockery of that crusade and of the deep American belief in human freedom and dignity which underlie it than to put the provisions of H. R. 9490 on our statute books.

I do not undertake lightly the responsibility of differing with the majority in both Houses of Congress who have voted for this bill. We are all Americans; we all wish to safeguard and preserve our constitutional liberties against internal and external enemies. But I cannot approve this legislation, which instead of accomplishing its avowed purpose would actually interfere with our liberties and help the Communists against whom the bill was aimed.

This is a time when we must marshal all our resources and all the moral strength of our free system in self-defense against the threat of Communist aggression. We will fail in this, and we will destroy all that we seek to preserve, if we sacrifice the liberties of our citizens in a misguided attempt to achieve national security.

There is no reason why we should fail. Our country has been through dangerous times before, without losing our liberties to external attack or internal hysteria. Each of us, in Government and out, has a share in guarding our liberties. Each of us must search his own conscience to find whether he is doing all that can be done to preserve and strengthen them.

No considerations of expediency can justify the enactment of such a bill as this, a bill which would so greatly weaken our liberties and give aid and comfort to those who would destroy us. I have, therefore, no alternative but to return this bill without my approval, and I earnestly request the Congress to reconsider its action.

HARRY S. TRUMAN.
The White House, September 22, 1950.

Sidney Hook:

ACADEMIC FREEDOM AND COMMUNISM

THE academic community through- out the United States is currently being disturbed by the perennial issue of the nature and limits of academic free- dom. The specific event which has pre- cipitated intense interest and discussion, not only in college classrooms but in all circles interested in education, is the ex- pulsion of some professors from the Uni- versity of Washington for being members of the Communist party. The arresting thing about this case is that for the first time in the history of education the grounds given for the expulsion of the professors is that *they* have been guilty of violating the principles of academic freedom, and therefore of "conduct un- becoming a teacher."

Here is certainly a startling reversal which reflects the emergence of new problems in culture and education not dreamed of when John Dewey and Arthur T. Lovejoy organized the Ameri- can Association of University Professors to further the interests of their profes- sion and defend academic freedom and tenure.

Because the decision may set an im- portant precedent in higher education, it invites a reconsideration of first princi- ples in the light of the facts.

If, as Cardinal Newman has observed, the function of a university is the dis- covery and publication of the truth in all branches of knowledge, then academic freedom is essential to its very life. For without the freedom to inquire, to chal- lenge and to doubt, truth cannot be well- grounded or error refuted. Since not everything which has been accepted is true, nor everything which is newly pro- posed is false, the result of inquiry some- times undermines the customary and supports the novel. When this takes place in non-controversial areas, it is recog- nized as the natural operation of the discipline of scientific inquiry; when it affects controversial issues, vested inter- ests and emotions are often aroused and attempts are made to safeguard some special doctrine and conclusion from the consequences of critical scrutiny.

Anything may be regarded as a con- troversial subject, from the heliocentric hypothesis and the theory of evolution to the causes of World War II and the wis- dom of the Marshall Plan. That is why universities from the time of their origin have been compelled to fight the battle for academic freedom over and over again. Although in the West, in matters of pure science, there are no longer powerful special interests that can be outraged by the progress of inquiry, in the social studies, arts and philosophy, convictions are not so clearly a function of evidence. Conclusions in these fields touch on issues of contemporary political or social concern in relation to which almost everyone believes he is something of an authority. One man's truth is often another man's propaganda.

Reprinted by special permission of Sidney Hook and *The New York Times Magazine*, February 27, 1949.

None the less no distinction in principle can be drawn between noncontroversial and controversial themes, especially if we recognize that all human judgments are fallible. The presumption is that university professors engaged in the search for truth are qualified by their professional competence. The judges of their competence can only be their intellectual peers or betters in their own fields. If this is denied, the university loses its *raison d'être* as an institution, not only for free research but critical teaching.

In consequence, any doctrinal impositions, no matter what their source, which set up limits beyond which the professor cannot go, affect him both as a scholar and a teacher. As a scholar, he loses professional standing in the intellectual community if it is suspected that his findings must fit the predetermined conclusions and prejudices of those whose first loyalty is not to the objective methods of seeing the truth. As a teacher, he cannot engage in the honest presentation and reasoned investigation of all relevant *alternatives* to the theories and policies he is considering. He runs the risk of forfeiting the respect of his students, who look to him for candid evaluation and intellectual stimulus, if they believe that he is time-serving or prudent beyond the call of scientific evidence.

If in the honest exercise of his academic freedom an individual reaches views which bring down about his head charges of "Communist," "Fascist" or what not, the academic community is duty bound to protect him irrespective of the truth of the charges. And since these words are often epithets of disparagement rather than of precise description, there is all the more reason why the university must stand firm. It places its faith in the loyalty of its teachers to the ethics and logic of scientific

inquiry. The heresies of yesterday are often the orthodoxies of today. In the interests of winning new truths, it is better to err on the side of toleration than of proscription.

This means that the professor occupies a position of trust not only in relation to the university and his student, but to the democratic community which places its faith and hope in the processes of education. ("If a nation expects to be ignorant and free, in a state of civilization," wrote Jefferson, "it expects what never was and what never will be.") Academic freedom therefore carries with it duties correlative with rights. No professor can violate them under the pretext that he is exercising his freedom. That is why the graduate faculty of the New School of Social Research explicitly declares that in the interests of academic freedom, "no member of the faculty can be a member of any political party or group which asserts the right to dictate in matters of science or scientific opinion."

So far the analysis of principles can take us. There remains the important question of fact. Is a member of the Communist party, so long as he remains a member, free to exercise his rights and fulfill his duties as an objective scholar and teacher? To answer this question we must look at what the Communist party itself teaches, its conditions of membership, and what has come to light about the actual behavior of known members of the Communist party. We are not dealing now with the right to hold Communist *beliefs* but with what is entailed by the *act* of membership in the Communist party as it affects educational practice.

First of all, it is important to recognize that there are no "sleepers" or passive members of the Communist party. The statutes of membership define a party member as one who not only "accepts the party program, attends the regular meetings of the membership branch of his place of work" but "who is *active* in party work." Inactivity as well as disagreement with the decisions of any party organization or committee are grounds for expulsion. The concluding sentence of the pledge which the member inducted into the Communist party takes since 1935 reads: "I pledge myself to remain at all times a vigilant and firm defender of the Leninist line of the party, the only line that insures the triumph of Soviet power in the United States." (Daily Worker, April 2, 1936)

The "place of work" of the Communist party teacher is the school or university. How is a Communist party member active in party work at the university? Here are some directives from the official organ of the Communist party (The Communist, May, 1937):

Party and Y. C. L. fractions set up within classes and departments must supplement and combat by means of discussions, brochures, etc., bourgeois omissions and distortions in the regular curriculum. *Marxist-Leninist analysis must be injected into every class.*

Communist teachers must take advantage of their positions, without exposing themselves, to give their students to the best of their ability working-class education.

To enable the teachers in the party to do the latter, the party must take careful steps to see that all teacher comrades are given thorough education in the teaching of Marxism-Leninism. Only when teachers have really mastered Marxism-Leninism will they be able skillfully to inject it into their teaching at the least risk of exposure and at the same time conduct struggles around the schools in a truly Bolshevik manner.

Two things are significant here. The first is the injunction to cooperate with Communist party fractions among students in order — I am still quoting from official sources —"*to guide and direct that spirit of rebelliousness which already exists.*" The practice, many years ago, was to organize Communist students and teachers in the same cells, but since this led to exposure when students dropped out, teachers and students are now separately organized and meet only through carefully selected committees.

The second noteworthy thing is that the Communist party teachers are fearful of exposure and quite aware that their practices violate accepted notions of academic freedom and responsibility. That is why when literature appears under their imprint it is anonymous. Since no one takes personal responsibility, what is said about things and persons, including non-Communist colleagues, is not likely to be scrupulous or accurate. Sometimes it is downright scurrilous.

How is it possible for the Communist party to control the thinking of its members who teach in so many different fields? What have literature, philosophy, science and mathematics got to do with its political program? The answer is to be found in the fact that according to the Communist party itself politics is bound up, through the class struggle, with every field of knowledge. On the basis of its philosophy of dialectical materialism, a party line is laid down for every area of thought from art to zoology. No person who is known to hold a view incompatible with the party line is accepted as a member. For example, if he is a historian he cannot become a member if he teaches that the economic factor is not the most decisive factor in history or, if a political scientist, that the state is not the executive committee of the ruling class or that the Soviet Union is not a democracy. Individuals have been denied membership in the Communist party because they did not believe in "dialectics" in nature.

If a philosopher, to cite cases from my own field, accepts the theories of Mach or Carnap or Husserl or Alexander or Dewey or T. H. Green or G. E. Moore, upon joining the Communist party he will criticize the doctrines he had espoused previously. He cannot ever criticize dialectical materialism or the theories of Lenin and Stalin whom he now regards as great philosophers. If a physicist or mathematician becomes a member of the Communist party he is required, wherever it is possible for him to do so, to relate his subject to the growth of technology, its impact upon social divisions, the class uses to which discovery is put, and the liberating role it can play in a Communist economy. The general theme is: science under capitalism makes for death and poverty; under communism, science makes for life and abundance.

The party line, however, is not constant in all fields. It changes with political exigencies. The life of a Communist party teacher, therefore, is not a happy one, since he may have to prove the opposite of what he once so fervently taught. His difficulties are mitigated by the fact that in different terms he faces different students whose memories are apt to be short in any event. But English teachers who have been members of the Communist party during the last few years have had to reverse their judgments about the same novelists, and sometimes even about the same books, e.g. Malraux's "Man's Fate," Dos Passos' "U.S.A.," Wright's "Native Son," because of changes in the party line toward these authors.

In the social sciences, Communist party teachers taught in 1934 that Roose-velt was a Fascist; in 1936, during the Popular Front, a progressive; in 1940, during the Nazi-Stalin Pact, a warmonger and imperialist; in 1941, after Hitler invaded the Soviet Union, a leader of the oppressed peoples of the world.

Whether with respect to specific issues Communist teachers have been right or wrong in these kaleidoscopic changes is not the relevant question. What is relevant is that their conclusions are not reached by a free inquiry into the evidence. To stay in the Communist party, they must believe and teach what the party line decrees. If anyone doubts this we have the objective evidence provided by Granville Hicks in his public letter of resignation from the Communist party. Hicks resigned because he was refused even the right *to suspend judgment* on the Nazi-Stalin pact. "If the party," he writes, "had left any room for doubt, I could go along with it . . . But they made it clear that if I eventually found it impossible to defend the pact, and defend it in their terms, there was nothing for me to do but resign." (New Republic, Oct. 4, 1939)

It is argued by some civil libertarians, who are prepared to grant the foregoing, that this is still not sufficient evidence to impugn the integrity of teachers who are members of the Communist party. They must be judged by their individual actions in the classroom; they must, so to speak, be "caught in the act" of inculcating the party line in the minds of their students.

This has two fatal difficulties. It would require spying in every classroom to detect the party line, and disorganize or intimidate not only Communist party members but the entire faculty, since a member of the Communist party admits membership only when faced with a charge of perjury, and not always then.

The academic community would wrathfully and rightfully repudiate any such practice.

Second, it would be very difficult to determine when a teacher was defending a conclusion because he honestly believed it followed from the evidence, and when he was carrying out his task as a good soldier in the party cause.

Those who contend that membership in the Communist party is *prima facie* evidence that a teacher does not believe in or practice academic freedom, insist that such membership is an *act,* not merely an expression of opinion. They deny that they are invoking the principle of guilt by association, for no one who joins and remains a member of the Communist party could be ignorant of what classroom practices are required of him. If he were ignorant, the Communist party itself would drop him for "inactivity."

It is interesting to note that this position is independent of the questions whether a teacher has a right to be a member of a legal party or whether the Communist party is or should be a legal organization. Paraphrasing Justice Holmes' famous remark about the Boston policeman, a man may have a constitutional right to be a member of the Communist party but he has no constitutional right to be a college professor unless he is free to accept the duties as well as rights of academic freedom. Anyone is free to join or leave the Communist party; but once he joins and remains a member, he is not a free mind.

Some administrative authorities have taken the position that they would not knowingly engage members of the Communist party, otherwise thought competent, but that they would not discharge them after they discovered the fact of their membership. This is obviously inconsistent. The reason which explains their reluctance to take on a member of the Communist party, if valid, still operates when he has already joined the faculty. If on educational grounds a Communist party member is objectionable *before* he has begun working for the party line, is he any less objectionable when he is actually in action? If anything, a person, known from the very outset as a member of the Communist party, may be assigned to a post where he can do far less damage than someone who has successfully concealed the fact of his membership.

There remains the question as to whether expulsion on grounds of membership in the Communist party does not set a dangerous precedent. Communists under fire in a sudden accession of concern for Catholics, express fear lest this threaten the tenure of teachers who are members of the Catholic Church.

As one who cannot be taxed with undue sympathy for Thomist doctrine, I should maintain there is no evidence whatsoever of the operation of Catholic cells in nonsectarian universities which impose a party line in all the arts and sciences that must be followed by all Catholic teachers on pain of excommunication. The comparison is a red herring. The danger to free inquiry in education from Catholic quarters comes not from teachers but from outside pressure groups.

If any other organization exists which operates like the Communist party, its members should be treated equitably with the members of the Communist party. Members of the Nazi party were under similar discipline. But in their case, before and after the Stalin-Hitler alliance, the Communists demanded their peremptory dismissal.

The problem of the "fellow-traveler" is

even a more difficult and involved question. But its solution, paradoxical as it may appear, is simple. It must be left entirely to the enlightened good sense of the academic community, which can apply various sanctions short of dismissal. The term "fellow-traveler" is hopelessly vague. "Fellow-travelers" come and go. They are of all varieties. No one is wise enough to pick out the dumb, innocent sheep from the cunning and dishonest goats. So long as they are not under the discipline of the Communist party, they may still be sensitive to the results of honest inquiry. Whatever harm they do is incomparably less than the harm that would result from any attempt to purge them. Without the steel core of the Communist party fraction on the campus to magnetize them, they will fly off in all the directions their scattered wits take them.

Although the exclusion of Communist party teachers from the academic community seems justified in *principle,* this by itself does not determine whether it is a wise or prudent action in *all* circumstances. Sometimes the consequences of removing an unmitigated evil may be such as to make its sufferance preferable. If removal of Communist party members were to be used by other reactionary elements as a pretext to hurl irresponsible charges against professors whose views they disapprove, a case might be made for suspending action. On the other hand, failure to act in a situation where the academic process has been flagrantly suborned may lead to public suspicion and reprisals that injure innocent and guilty alike.

How to protect the innocent, as well as those who have genuinely broken with the Communist party, from dangers attending a policy justified in principle is too large a theme to explore here. But I am confident that *if the execution of the policy were left to university faculties themselves,* and not to administrators and trustees who are harried by pressure groups, there would be little ground for complaint. In the last analysis there is no safer repository of the integrity of teaching and scholarship than the dedicated men and women who constitute the faculties of our colleges and universities.

Alexander Meiklejohn:

SHOULD COMMUNISTS BE ALLOWED TO TEACH?

THE president and regents of the University of Washington have dismissed three professors and have placed three others on probation. That statement fails to mention the most significant feature of what has been done. The entire faculty is now on probation. Every scholar, every teacher, is officially notified that if, in his search for the truth, he finds the policies of the American

From *The New York Times Magazine,* March 27, 1949. Used by permission.

Communist party to be wise, and acts on that belief, he will be dismissed from the university.

In one of the dismissal cases, the evidence is not clear enough to enable an outsider to measure the validity of the decision. But the other five cases force an issue on which everyone who cares for the integrity and freedom of American scholarship and teaching must take his stand. Cool and careful consideration of that issue should be given by all of us, whether or not we agree with the teachers in question, but especially if we do not agree with them.

The general question in dispute is that of the meaning of academic freedom. But that question has three distinct phases. The first of these has to do with the organization of a university. It asks about the rights and duties of the faculty in relation to the rights and duties of the administration. And the principle at issue corresponds closely to that which, in the Government of the United States, is laid down by the First Amendment to the Constitution. Just as that Amendment declares that "Congress shall make no law abridging the freedom of speech," so, generally, our universities and colleges have adopted a principle which forbids the administration to abridge the intellectual freedom of scholars and teachers. And, at this point, the question is whether or not the president and regents at Washington have violated an agreement, made in good faith, and of vital importance to the work of the university.

The principle of academic freedom was clearly stated by Sidney Hook in The New York Times Magazine of Feb. 27, 1949. After noting that "administrators and trustees" are "harried by pressure-groups," Mr. Hook concluded his argument by saying, "In the last analysis,

there is no safer repository of the integrity of teaching and scholarship than the dedicated men and women who constitute the faculties of our colleges and universities." On the basis of that conviction, the Association of University Professors has advocated, and most of our universities, including Washington, have adopted, a "tenure system." That system recognizes that legal authority to appoint, promote, and dismiss teachers belongs to the president and regents. But so far as dismissals are concerned, the purpose of the tenure agreement is to set definite limits to the exercise of that authority.

This limitation of their power, governing boards throughout the nation have gladly recognized and accepted. To the Association of University Professors it has seemed so important that violations of it have been held to justify a "blacklisting" of a transgressor institution — a recommendation by the association that scholars and teachers refuse to serve in a university or college which has thus broken down the defenses of free inquiry and belief.

It is essential at this point to note the fact that the fear expressed by the tenure system is a fear of action by the president and regents. Since these officers control the status and the salaries of teachers, it is only through them or by them that effective external pressure can be used to limit faculty freedom. To say, then, as we must, that the explicit purpose of the tenure system is to protect freedom against the president and regents, is not to say that these officials are more evil than others. It says only that they are more powerful than others. Theirs is the power by which, unless it is checked by a tenure system, evil may be done.

Under the excellent code adopted at the University of Washington, it is agreed that, after a trial period in which the university makes sure that a teacher is competent and worthy of confidence, he is given "permanence" of tenure. This means that he is secure from dismissal unless one or more of five carefully specified charges are proved against him. And the crucial feature of this defense of freedom is that the holding of any set of opinions, however unpopular or unconventional, is scrupulously excluded from the list of proper grounds for dismissal. The teacher who has tenure may, therefore, go fearlessly wherever his search for the truth may lead him. And no officer of the university has authority, openly or by indirection, to abridge that freedom.

When, under the Washington code, charges are made against a teacher, it is provided that prosecution and defense shall be heard by a tenure committee of the faculty, which shall judge whether or not the accusations have been established. In the five cases here under discussion, the only charge made was that of present or past membership in the American Communist party. Specific evidence of acts revealing unfitness or misconduct in university or other activities was deliberately excluded from the prosecution case. And, further, since the alleged fact of party membership was frankly admitted by the defense, the only question at issue was the abstract inquiry whether or not such membership is forbidden under the five provisions of the tenure code.

Upon that issue, the faculty committee decided unanimously that, in the cases of the ex-members of the Communist party, there were, under the code, no grounds for dismissal. And, by a vote of eight to three, the same conclusion was reached concerning the two men who were still members of the party. In the discussions of the committee, the suggestion was made that the code should be so amended that party membership would give ground for dismissal. But that action was not recommended. In its capacity as the interpreter of the code which now protects academic freedom, the committee, in all five cases, declared the charges to be not supported by the evidence presented.

In response to this judgment upon teachers by their intellectual peers, the regents, on recommendation of the president, dismissed the two party members. And, second, going beyond the recommendation of the president, they placed the three ex-members "on probation" for two years. These actions are clearly a violation of the agreement under which faculty members have accepted or continued service in the university. They deserve the condemnation of everyone who respects the integrity of a covenant, of everyone who values faculty freedom and faculty responsibility for the maintaining of freedom.

The second phase of the general question goes deeper than the forms of university organization. It challenges the wisdom of the tenure code as it now stands. It may be that, though the regents are wrong in procedure, they are right in principle. Here, then, we must ask whether President Allen is justified in saying that a teacher who is "sincere in his belief in communism" cannot "at the same time be a sincere seeker after truth which is the first obligation of the teacher." In a press interview, Mr. Allen is quoted as saying, "I insist that the Communist party exercises thought control over every one of its members. That's what I object to." Such teachers, he tells us, are "incompetent, intellectually dishonest, and derelict in their duty to find and teach the truth." Can those assertions be verified? If so, then the tenure code should be amended. If not, then the action of the university should be immediately and decisively reversed.

No one can deny that a member of the American Communist party accepts a "discipline." He follows a party "line." As the policies of the party shift, he shifts with them. That statement is in some measure true of all parties, whose members agree to work together by common tactics toward a common end. But the Communist discipline, it must be added, is unusually rigid and severe. Our question is, then, whether submission to that discipline unfits for university work men who, on grounds of scholarship and character, have been judged by their colleagues to be fitted for it.

For the judging of that issue we must examine the forces by means of which the discipline of the American Communist party is exercised. It is idle to speak of "thought control" except as we measure the compulsions by which that control is made effective. What, then, are the inducements, the dominations which, by their impact upon the minds of these university teachers, rob them of the scholar's proper objectivity?

So far as inducements are concerned, good measuring of them requires that we place side by side the advantages offered to a scholar by the Communist party and those offered by the president and regents of a university. On the one hand, as seen in the present case, the administration can break a man's career at one stroke. It has power over every external thing he cares for. It can destroy his means of livelihood, can thwart his deepest inclinations and intentions. For example, in very many of our universities it is today taken for granted that a young scholar who is known to be a Communist has not the slightest chance of a faculty appointment. He is barred from aca-

demic work. And, as against this, what has the American Communist party to offer? Its "inducements" are the torments of suspicion, disrepute, insecurity, personal and family disaster.

Why, then, do men and women of scholarly training and taste choose party membership? Undoubtedly, some of them are, hysterically, attracted by disrepute and disaster. But, in general, the only explanation which fits the facts is that these scholars are moved by a passionate determination to follow the truth where it seems to lead, no matter what may be the cost to themselves and their families. If anyone wishes to unearth the "inducements" which threaten the integrity of American scholarship he can find far more fruitful lines of inquiry than that taken by the administration of the University of Washington.

But Communist controls, we are told, go far deeper than "inducements." The members of the party, it is said, "take orders from Moscow"; they are subject to "thought control by a foreign power." Now, here again, the fact of rigid party discipline makes these assertions, in some ambiguous sense, true. But, in the sense in which President Allen and his regents interpret them, they are radically false.

Let us assume as valid the statement that, in the American Communist party "orders" do come from Moscow. But by what power are those orders enforced in the United States? In the Soviet Union, Mr. Stalin and his colleagues can, and do, enforce orders by police and military might. In that nation their control is violent and dictatorial. But by what form of "might" do they control an American teacher in an American university? What can they do to him? At its extreme limit, their only enforcing action is that of dismissal from the party. They can say to him, "You cannot be a member of this party unless you believe our doctrines, unless you conform to our policies." But, under that form of control, a man's acceptance of doctrines and policies is not "required." It is voluntary.

To say that beliefs are required as "conditions of membership" in a party is not to say that the beliefs are required by force, unless it is shown that membership in the party is enforced. If membership is free, then the beliefs are free.

Misled by the hatreds and fears of the cold war, President Allen and his regents are unconsciously tricked by the ambiguities of the words, "control," and "require," and "free" and "objective." The scholars whom they condemn are, so far as the evidence shows free American citizens. For purposes of social action, they have chosen party affiliation with other men, here and abroad, whose beliefs are akin to their own. In a word, they do not accept Communist beliefs because they are members of the party. They are members of the party because they accept Communist beliefs.

Specific evidence to support the assertion just made was staring President Allen and his regents in the face at the very time when they were abstractedly denying that such evidence could exist. Three of the five men whom they condemned as enslaved by party orders had already, by their own free and independent thinking, resigned from the party. How could they have done that if, as charged, they were incapable of free and independent thinking? Slaves do not resign.

At the committee hearings, these men explained, simply and directly, that, under past conditions, they had found the party the most effective available weapon for attack upon evil social forces but that, with changing conditions, the use of that weapon seemed no longer advisable. Shall we say that the decision to be in the party gave evidence of a lack of objectivity while the decision to resign gave evidence of the possession of it? Such a statement would have no meaning except as indicating our own lack of objectivity.

In these three cases, as in the more famous case of Granville Hicks who, some years ago, resigned party membership with a brilliant account of his reasons for doing so, the charge made cannot be sustained. The accusation as it stands means nothing more than that the president and regents are advocating one set of ideas and are banning another. They are attributing to their victims their own intellectual sins. And the tragedy of their action is that it has immeasurably injured the cause which they seek to serve and, correspondingly, has advanced the cause which they are seeking to hold back.

The third phase of our question has to do with the wisdom, the effectiveness, of the educational policy under which teachers have been dismissed or put on probation. And, on this issue, the evidence against the president and regents is clear and decisive. However good their intention, they have made a fatal blunder in teaching method.

As that statement is made, it is taken for granted that the primary task of education in our colleges and universities is the teaching of the theory and practice of intellectual freedom, as the first principle of the democratic way of life. Whatever else our students may do or fail to do, they must learn what freedom is. They must learn to believe in it, to love it, and most important of all, to trust it.

What, then, is this faith in freedom, so far as the conflict of opinions is concerned? With respect to the world-wide controversy now raging between the advocates of the freedom of belief and the advocates of suppression of belief, what is our American doctrine? Simply stated, that doctrine expresses our confidence that whenever, in the field of ideas, the advocates of freedom and the advocates of suppression meet in fair and unabridged discussion, freedom will win. If that were not true, if the intellectual program of democracy could not hold its own in fair debate, then that program itself would require of us its own abandonment. That chance we believers in self-government have determined to take. We have put our faith in democracy.

But the president and regents have, at this point, taken the opposite course. They have gone over to the enemy. They are not willing to give a fair and equal hearing to those who disagree with us. They are convinced that suppression is more effective as an agency of freedom than is freedom itself.

But this procedure violates the one basic principle on which all teaching rests. It is impossible to teach what one does not believe. It is idle to preach what one does not practice. These men who advocate that we do to the Russians what the Russians, if they had the power, would do to us are declaring that the Russians are right and that we are wrong. They practice suppression, because they have more faith in the methods of dictatorship than in those of a free self-governing society.

For many years the writer of these words has watched the disastrous educational effects upon student opinion and attitude when suppression has been used, openly or secretly, in our universities and colleges. The outcome is always the same. Dictatorship breeds rebellion and dissatisfaction. High-spirited youth will not stand the double-dealing which prates of academic freedom and muzzles its teach-

ers by putting them "on probation."

If we suggest to these young people that they believe in democracy, then they will insist on knowing what can be said against it as well as what can be said for it. If we ask them to get ready to lay down their lives in conflict against an enemy, they want to know not only how strong or how weak are the military forces of that enemy, but also what he has to say for himself as against what we are saying for ourselves.

Many of the students in our colleges and universities are today driven into an irresponsible radicalism. But that drive does not come from the critics of our American political institutions. It comes chiefly from the irresponsible defenders of those institutions — the men who make a mockery of freedom by using in its service the forces of suppression.

Underlying and surrounding the Washington controversy is the same controversy as it runs through our national life. The most tragic mistake of the contemporary American mind is its failure to recognize the inherent strength and stability of free institutions when they are true to themselves. Democracy is not a weak and unstable thing which forever needs propping up by the devices of dictatorship. It is the only form of social life and of government which today has assurance of maintaining itself.

As contrasted with it, all governments of suppression are temporary and insecure. The regimes of Hitler and Mussolini flared into strength, and quickly died away. The power of the Soviet Union cannot endure unless that nation can find its way into the practices of political freedom. And all the other dictatorships are falling, and will fall, day by day. Free self-government alone gives promise of permanence and peace. The only real danger which threatens our democracy is that lack of faith which leads us into the devices and follies of suppression.*

* Attention is directed to Sidney Hook's article, "Academic Integrity and Academic Freedom" (*Commentary*, Vol. 8, Oct. 1949, pp. 329–339), in which Professor Hook specifically replies to Dr. Meiklejohn's article. Meiklejohn is wrong, says Hook, in expecting "fair and unabridged discussion" of any issue from Communists because party-membership is visible proof that loyalty to the Soviet regime is superior to loyalty to truth. It is proof of intellectual dishonesty because it signifies an agreement to teach *"according to directives received* and not in accordance with objective methods of searching for the truth. . . . It is precisely this subordination to his total commitment, and his evaluation of what is important or unimportant in the light of a political objective, that makes it impossible for him to exercise the free criticism he would engage in were he loyal to the principles of scientific inquiry."* Thus, according to Hook, while Meiklejohn may be correct in saying a member "freely" joined the Party, he is utterly wrong in saying the member "freely" holds the beliefs he publicly expresses. Ed.

Henry Steele Commager:

WHO IS LOYAL TO AMERICA?

O N May 6 a Russian-born girl, Mrs. Shura Lewis, gave a talk to the students of the Western High School of Washington, D. C. She talked about Russia — its school system, its public health program, the position of women, of the aged, of the workers, the farmers, and the professional classes — and compared, superficially and uncritically, some American and Russian social institutions. The most careful examination of the speech — happily reprinted for us in the *Congressional Record* — does not disclose a single disparagement of anything American unless it is a quasi-humorous reference to the cost of having a baby and of dental treatment in this country. Mrs. Lewis said nothing that had not been said a thousand times, in speeches, in newspapers, magazines, and books. She said nothing that any normal person could find objectionable.

Her speech, however, created a sensation. A few students walked out on it. Others improvised placards proclaiming their devotion to Americanism. Indignant mothers telephoned their protests. Newspapers took a strong stand against the outrage. Congress, rarely concerned for the political or economic welfare of the citizens of the capital city, reacted sharply when its intellectual welfare was at stake. Congressmen Rankin and Dirksen thundered and lightened; the District of Columbia Committee went into a huddle; there were demands for housecleaning in the whole school system, which was obviously shot through and through with Communism.

All this might be ignored, for we have learned not to expect either intelligence or understanding of Americanism from this element in our Congress. More ominous was the reaction of the educators entrusted with the high responsibility of guiding and guarding the intellectual

From *Harper's Magazine*, Vol. 195, No. 1168 (September, 1947). Used by permission.

welfare of our boys and girls. Did they stand up for intellectual freedom? Did they insist that high-school children had the right and the duty to learn about other countries? Did they protest that students were to be trusted to use intelligence and common sense? Did they affirm that the Americanism of their students was staunch enough to resist propaganda? Did they perform even the elementary task, expected of educators above all, of analyzing the much-criticized speech?

Not at all. The District Superintendent of Schools, Dr. Hobart Corning, hastened to agree with the animadversions of Representatives Rankin and Dirksen. The whole thing was, he confessed, "a very unfortunate occurrence," and had "shocked the whole school system." What Mrs. Lewis said, he added gratuitously, was "repugnant to all who are working with youth in the Washington schools," and "the entire affair contrary to the philosophy of education under which we operate." Mr. Danowsky, the hapless principal of the Western High School, was "the most shocked and regretful of all." The District of Columbia Committee would be happy to know that though he was innocent in the matter, he had been properly reprimanded!

It is the reaction of the educators that makes this episode more than a tempest in a teapot. We expect hysteria from Mr. Rankin and some newspapers; we are shocked when we see educators, timid before criticism and confused about first principles, betray their trust. And we wonder what can be that "philosophy of education" which believes that young people can be trained to the duties of citizenship by wrapping their minds in cotton-wool.

Merely by talking about Russia Mrs.

Lewis was thought to be attacking Americanism. It is indicative of the seriousness of the situation that during this same week the House found it necessary to take time out from the discussion of the labor bill, the tax bill, the International Trade Organization, and the world famine, to meet assaults upon Americanism from a new quarter. This time it was the artists who were undermining the American system, and members of the House spent some hours passing around reproductions of the paintings which the State Department had sent abroad as part of its program for advertising American culture. We need not pause over the exquisite humor which congressmen displayed in their comments on modern art: weary statesmen must have their fun. But we may profitably remark the major criticism which was directed against this unfortunate collection of paintings. What was wrong with these paintings, it shortly appeared, was that they were un-American. "No American drew those crazy pictures," said Mr. Rankin. Perhaps he was right. The copious files of the Committee on Un-American Activities were levied upon to prove that of the forty-five artists represented "no less than twenty were definitely New Deal in various shades of Communism." The damning facts are specified for each of the pernicious twenty; we can content ourselves with the first of them, Ben-Zion. What is the evidence here? "Ben-Zion was one of the signers of a letter sent to President Roosevelt by the United American Artists which urged help to the USSR and Britain after Hitler attacked Russia." He was, in short, a fellow-traveler of Churchill and Roosevelt.

The same day that Mr. Dirksen was denouncing the Washington school authorities for allowing students to hear about Russia ("In Russia equal right is granted to each nationality. There is no discrimination. Nobody says, you are a Negro, you are a Jew") Representative Williams of Mississippi rose to denounce the *Survey-Graphic* magazine and to add further to our understanding of Americanism. The *Survey-Graphic,* he said, "contained 129 pages of outrageously vile and nauseating anti-Southern, anti-Christian, un-American, and pro-Communist tripe, ostensibly directed toward the elimination of the custom of racial segregation in the South." It was written by "meddling un-American purveyors of hate and indecency."

All in all, a busy week for the House. Yet those who make a practice of reading their *Record* will agree that it was a typical week. For increasingly Congress is concerned with the eradication of disloyalty and the defense of Americanism, and scarcely a day passes that some congressman does not treat us to exhortations and admonitions, impassioned appeals and eloquent declamations, similar to those inspired by Mrs. Lewis, Mr. Ben-Zion, and the editors of the *Survey-Graphic.* And scarcely a day passes that the outlines of the new loyalty and the new Americanism are not etched more sharply in public policy.

And this is what is significant — the emergence of new patterns of Americanism and of loyalty, patterns radically different from those which have long been traditional. It is not only the Congress that is busy designing the new patterns. They are outlined in President Truman's recent disloyalty order; in similar orders formulated by the New York City Council and by state and local authorities throughout the country; in the programs of the D.A.R., the American Legion, and similar patriotic organizations; in the edi-

torials of the Hearst and the McCormick-Patterson papers; and in an elaborate series of advertisements sponsored by large corporations and business organizations. In the making is a revival of the red hysteria of the early 1920's, one of the shabbiest chapters in the history of American democracy; and more than a revival, for the new crusade is designed not merely to frustrate Communism but to formulate a positive definition of Americanism, and a positive concept of loyalty.

What is the new loyalty? It is, above all, conformity. It is the uncritical and unquestioning acceptance of America as it is — the political institutions, the social relationships, the economic practices. It rejects inquiry into the race question or socialized medicine, or public housing, or into the wisdom or validity of our foreign policy. It regards as particularly heinous any challenge to what is called "the system of private enterprise," identifying that system with Americanism. It abandons evolution, repudiates the once popular concept of progress, and regards America as a finished product, perfect and complete.

It is, it must be added, easily satisfied. For it wants not intellectual conviction nor spiritual conquest, but mere outward conformity. In matters of loyalty it takes the word for the deed, the gesture for the principle. It is content with the flag salute, and does not pause to consider the warning of our Supreme Court that "a person gets from a symbol the meaning he puts into it, and what is one man's comfort and inspiration is another's jest and scorn." It is satisfied with membership in respectable organizations and, as it assumes that every member of a liberal organization is a Communist, concludes that every member of a conservative one is a true American. It has not yet learned that not everyone who saith Lord, Lord, shall enter into the kingdom of Heaven. It is designed neither to discover real disloyalty nor to foster true loyalty.

II

What is wrong with this new concept of loyalty? What, fundamentally, is wrong with the pusillanimous retreat of the Washington educators, the barbarous antics of Washington legislators, the hysterical outbursts of the D.A.R., the gross and vulgar appeals of business corporations? It is not merely that these things are offensive. It is rather that they are wrong — morally, socially, and politically.

The concept of loyalty as conformity is a false one. It is narrow and restrictive, denies freedom of thought and of conscience, and is irremediably stained by private and selfish considerations. "Enlightened loyalty," wrote Josiah Royce, who made loyalty the very core of his philosophy,

means harm to no man's loyalty. It is at war only with disloyalty, and its warfare, unless necessity constrains, is only a spiritual warfare. It does not foster class hatreds; it knows of nothing reasonable about race prejudices; and it regards all races of men as one in their need of loyalty. It ignores mutual misunderstandings. It loves its own wherever upon earth its own, namely loyalty itself, is to be found.

Justice, charity, wisdom, spirituality, he added, were all definable in terms of loyalty, and we may properly ask which of these qualities our contemporary champions of loyalty display.

Above all, loyalty must be to something larger than oneself, untainted by private purposes or selfish ends. But what are we to say of the attempts by the NAM and by individual corporations to identify loyalty with the system of private enterprise? Is it not as if officeholders should attempt to identify loyalty with their own party, their own political careers? Do not those corporations which pay for full-page advertisements associating Americanism with the competitive system expect, ultimately, to profit from that association? Do not those organizations that deplore, in the name of patriotism, the extension of government operation of hydro-electric power expect to profit from their campaign?

Certainly it is a gross perversion not only of the concept of loyalty but of the concept of Americanism to identify it with a particular economic system. This precise question, interestingly enough, came before the Supreme Court in the Schneiderman case not so long ago — and it was Wendell Willkie who was counsel for Schneiderman. Said the Court:

Throughout our history many sincere people whose attachment to the general Constitutional scheme cannot be doubted have, for various and even divergent reasons, urged differing degrees of governmental ownership and control of natural resources, basic means of production, and banks and the media of exchange, either with or without compensation. And something once regarded as a species of private property was abolished without compensating the owners when the institution of slavery was forbidden. Can it be said that the author of the Emancipation Proclamation and the supporters of the Thirteenth Amendment were not attached to the Constitution?

There is, it should be added, a further danger in the willful identification of Americanism with a particular body of economic practices. Many learned economists predict for the near future an economic crash similar to that of 1929. If Americanism is equated with competitive capitalism, what happens to it if competitive capitalism comes a cropper? If loyalty and private enterprise are inextricably associated, what is to preserve loyalty if private enterprise fails? Those who associate Americanism with a particular program of economic practices have a grave responsibility, for if their program should fail, they expose Americanism itself to disrepute.

The effort to equate loyalty with conformity is misguided because it assumes that there is a fixed content to loyalty and that this can be determined and defined. But loyalty is a principle, and eludes definition except in its own terms. It is devotion to the best interests of the commonwealth, and may require hostility to the particular policies which the government pursues, the particular practices which the economy undertakes, the particular institutions which society maintains. "If there is any fixed star in our Constitutional constellation," said the Supreme Court in the Barnette case, "it is that no official, high or petty, can prescribe what shall be orthodox in politics, nationalism, religion, or other matters of opinion, or force citizens to confess by word or act their faith therein. If there are any circumstances which permit an exception they do not now occur to us."

True loyalty may require, in fact, what appears to the naïve to be disloyalty. It may require hostility to certain provisions of the Constitution itself, and historians have not concluded that those who subscribed to the "Higher Law" were lacking in patriotism. We should not forget that our tradition is one of protest and revolt, and it is stultifying to celebrate the rebels of the past — Jefferson and Paine, Emerson and Thoreau — while we silence the rebels of the present. "We are a rebellious nation," said Theodore Parker, known in his day as the Great American Preacher, and went on:

Our whole history is treason; our blood was attainted before we were born; our creeds are infidelity to the mother church; our constitution, treason to our fatherland. What of that? Though all the governors in the world bid us commit treason against man, and set the example, let us never submit.

Those who would impose upon us a new concept of loyalty not only assume that this is possible, but have the presumption to believe that they are competent to write the definition. We are reminded of Whitman's defiance of the "never-ending audacity of elected persons." Who are those who would set the standards of loyalty? They are Rankins and Bilbos, officials of the D.A.R. and the Legion and the NAM, Hearsts and McCormicks. May we not say of Rankin's harangues on loyalty what Emerson said of Webster at the time of the Seventh of March speech: "The word honor in the mouth of Mr. Webster is like the word love in the mouth of a whore."

What do men know of loyalty who make a mockery of the Declaration of Independence and the Bill of Rights, whose energies are dedicated to stirring up race and class hatreds, who would straitjacket the American spirit? What indeed do they know of America — the America of Sam Adams and Tom Paine, of Jackson's defiance of the Court and Lincoln's celebration of labor, of Thoreau's essay on Civil Disobedience and Emerson's championship of John Brown, of the America of the Fourierists and the Come-Outers, of cranks and fanatics, of socialists and anarchists? Who among American heroes could meet their tests, who would be cleared by their committees? Not Washington, who was a rebel. Not Jefferson, who wrote that all men are created equal and whose motto was "rebellion to tyrants is obedience to God." Not Garrison, who publicly burned the

Constitution; or Wendell Phillips, who spoke for the underprivileged everywhere and counted himself a philosophical anarchist; not Seward of the Higher Law or Sumner of racial equality. Not Lincoln, who admonished us to have malice toward none, charity for all; or Wilson, who warned that our flag was "a flag of liberty of opinion as well as of political liberty"; or Justice Holmes, who said that our Constitution is an experiment and that while that experiment is being made "we should be eternally vigilant against attempts to check the expression of opinions that we loathe and believe to be fraught with death."

III

There are further and more practical objections against the imposition of fixed concepts of loyalty or tests of disloyalty. The effort is itself a confession of fear, a declaration of insolvency. Those who are sure of themselves do not need reassurance, and those who have confidence in the strength and the virtue of America do not need to fear either criticism or competition. The effort is bound to miscarry. It will not apprehend those who are really disloyal, it will not even frighten them; it will affect only those who can be labeled "radical." It is sobering to recall that though the Japanese relocation program, carried through at such incalculable cost in misery and tragedy, was justified to us on the ground that the Japanese were potentially disloyal, the record does not disclose a single case of Japanese disloyalty or sabotage during the whole war. The warning sounded by the Supreme Court in the Barnette flag-salute case is a timely one:

Ultimate futility of such attempts to compel obedience is the lesson of every such effort from the Roman drive to stamp out

Christianity as a disturber of pagan unity, the Inquisition as a means to religious and dynastic unity, the Siberian exiles as a means to Russian unity, down to the fast-failing efforts of our present totalitarian enemies. Those who begin coercive elimination of dissent soon find themselves exterminating dissenters. Compulsory unification of opinion achieves only the unanimity of the graveyard.

Nor are we left to idle conjecture in this matter; we have had experience enough. Let us limit ourselves to a single example, one that is wonderfully relevant. Back in 1943 the House Un-American Activities Committee, deeply disturbed by alleged disloyalty among government employees, wrote a definition of subversive activities and proceeded to apply it. The definition was admirable, and no one could challenge its logic or its symmetry:

Subversive activity derives from conduct intentionally destructive of or inimical to the Government of the United States — that which seeks to undermine its institutions, or to distort its functions, or to impede its projects, or to lessen its efforts, the ultimate end being to overturn it all.

Surely anyone guilty of activities so defined deserved not only dismissal but punishment. But how was the test applied? It was applied to two distinguished scholars, Robert Morss Lovett and Goodwin Watson, and to one able young historian, William E. Dodd, Jr., son of our former Ambassador to Germany. Of almost three million persons employed by the government, these were the three whose subversive activities were deemed the most pernicious, and the House cut them off the payroll. The sequel is familiar. The Senate concurred only to save a wartime appropriation; the President signed the bill under protest for the same reason. The Supreme Court declared the whole business a "bill of attainder" and therefore unconstitutional. Who was it, in the end, who engaged in "subversive activities" — Lovett, Dodd, and Watson, or the Congress which flagrantly violated Article One of the Constitution?

Finally, disloyalty tests are not only futile in application, they are pernicious in their consequences. They distract attention from activities that are really disloyal, and silence criticism inspired by true loyalty. That there are disloyal elements in America will not be denied, but there is no reason to suppose that any of the tests now formulated will ever be applied to them. It is relevant to remember that when Rankin was asked why his Committee did not investigate the Ku Klux Klan he replied that the Klan was not un-American, it was American!

Who are those who are really disloyal? Those who inflame racial hatreds, who sow religious and class dissensions. Those who subvert the Constitution by violating the freedom of the ballot box. Those who make a mockery of majority rule by the use of the filibuster. Those who impair democracy by denying equal educational facilities. Those who frustrate justice by lynch law or by making a farce of jury trials. Those who deny freedom of speech and of the press and of assembly. Those who press for special favors against the interest of the commonwealth. Those who regard public office as a source of private gain. Those who would exalt the military over the civil. Those who for selfish and private purposes stir up national antagonisms, and expose the world to the ruin of war.

Will the House Committee on Un-American Activities interfere with the activities of these? Will Mr. Truman's disloyalty proclamation reach these? Will the current campaigns for Americanism convert these? If past experience is any guide, they will not. What they will do, if they are successful, is to silence criticism, stamp out dissent — or drive it underground. But if our democracy is to flourish it must have criticism, if our government is to function it must have dissent. Only totalitarian governments insist upon conformity and they — as we know — do so at their peril. Without criticism abuses will go unrebuked; without dissent our dynamic system will become static. The American people have a stake in the maintenance of the most thorough-going inquisition into American institutions. They have a stake in nonconformity, for they know that the American genius is nonconformist. They have a stake in experimentation of the most radical character, for they know that only those who prove all things can hold fast that which is good.

IV

It is easier to say what loyalty is not than to say what it is. It is not conformity. It is not passive acquiescence in the status quo. It is not preference for everything American over everything foreign. It is not an ostrich-like ignorance of other countries and other institutions. It is not the indulgence in ceremony — a flag salute, an oath of allegiance, a fervid verbal declaration. It is not a particular creed, a particular version of history, a particular body of economic practices, a particular philosophy.

It is a tradition, an ideal, and a principle. It is a willingness to subordinate every private advantage for the larger good. It is an appreciation of the rich and diverse contributions that can come from the most varied sources. It is allegiance to the traditions that have guided our greatest statesmen and inspired our most eloquent poets – the traditions of freedom, equality, democracy, tolerance, the tradition of the higher law, of experimentation, co-operation, and pluralism. It is a realization that America was born of revolt, flourished on dissent, became great through experimentation.

Independence was an act of revolution; republicanism was something new under the sun; the federal system was a vast experimental laboratory. Physically Americans were pioneers; in the realm of social and economic institutions, too, their tradition has been one of pioneering. From the beginning, intellectual and spiritual diversity have been as characteristic of America as racial and linguistic. The most distinctively American philosophies have been transcendentalism – which is the philosophy of the Higher Law – and pragmatism – which is the philosophy of experimentation and pluralism. These two principles are the very core of Americanism: the principle of the Higher Law, or of obedience to the dictates of conscience rather than of statutes, and the principle of pragmatism, or the rejection of a single good and of the notion of a finished universe. From the beginning Americans have known that there were new worlds to conquer, new truths to be discovered. Every effort to confine Americanism to a single pattern, to constrain it to a single formula, is disloyalty to everything that is valid in Americanism.

J. Edgar Hoover:

THE DISLOYALTY OF COMMUNISTS AND FELLOW TRAVELERS

THE Communist movement in the United States began to manifest itself in 1919. Since then it has changed its name and its party line whenever expedient and tactical. But always it comes back to fundamentals and bills itself as the party of Marxism-Leninism. As such, it stands for the destruction of our American form of government; it stands for the destruction of American democracy; it stands for the destruction of free enterprise; and it stands for the creation of a "Soviet of the United States" and ultimate world revolution. . . .

In recent years, the Communists have been very cautious about using such phrases as "force and violence"; nevertheless, it is the subject of much discussion in their schools and in party caucus where they readily admit that the only way in which they can defeat the present ruling class is by world revolution.

Testimony of J. Edgar Hoover, Director, Federal Bureau of Investigation, before the Committee on Un-American Activities, House of Representatives, 80th Congress, 1st session, on H. R. 1884 and H. R. 2122, March 26, 1947.

The Communist, once he is fully trained and indoctrinated, realizes that he can create his order in the United States only by "bloody revolution."

Their chief textbook, The History of the Communist Party of the Soviet Union, is used as a basis for planning their revolution. Their tactics require that to be successful they must have:

1. The will and sympathy of the people.

2. Military aid and assistance.

3. Plenty of guns and ammunition.

4. A program for extermination of the police as they are the most important enemy and are termed "trained Fascists."

5. Seizure of all communications, busses, railroads, radio stations, and other forms of communications and transportation.

They evade the question of force and violence publicly. They hold that when Marxists speak of force and violence they will not be responsible — that force and violence will be the responsibility of their enemies. They adopt the novel premise that they do not advocate force and violence publicly but that when their class resists to defend themselves then they are thus accused of using force and violence. A lot of double talk. . . .

The Party Line

The Communist Party line changes from day to day. The one cardinal rule that can always be applied to what the party line is or will be is found in the fundamental principle of Communist teachings that the support of Soviet Russia is the duty of Communists of all countries.

One thing is certain. The American progress which all good citizens seek, such as old-age security, houses for veterans, child assistance and a host of others is being adopted as window dressing by the Communists to conceal their true aims and entrap gullible followers. . . .

Strength of the Party

. . . The numerical strength of the party's enrolled membership is insignificant. But it is well known that there are many actual members who because of their position are not carried on party rolls. . . .

What is important is the claim of the Communists themselves that for every party member there are 10 others ready, willing, and able to do the party's work. . . .

One who accepts the aims, principles, and program of the party, who attends meetings, who reads the party press and literature, who pays dues and who is active on behalf of the party "shall be considered a member." The open, avowed Communist who carries a card and pays dues is no different from a security standpoint than the person who does the party's work but pays no dues, carries no card and is not on the party rolls. In fact, the latter is a greater menace because of his opportunity to work in stealth.

Identifying Undercover Communists, Fellow Travelers, and Sympathizers

The burden of proof is placed upon those who consistently follow the ever-changing, twisting party line. Fellow travelers and sympathizers can deny party membership but they can never escape the undeniable fact that they have played into the Communist hands, thus furthering the Communist cause by playing the role of innocent, gullible, or willful allies.

Propaganda Activities

. . . The Communist propaganda technique is designed to promote emotional response with the hope that the victim will be attracted by what he is told the Communist way of life holds in store for him. The objective, of course, is to develop discontent and hasten the day when the Communists can gather sufficient support and following to overthrow the American way of life.

Communist propaganda is always slanted in the hope that the Communist may be alined with liberal progressive causes. The honest liberal and progressive should be alert to this, and I believe the Communists' most effective foes can be the real liberals and progressives who understand their devious machinations. . . .

Correspondence Campaigns

Communists and their followers are prolific letter writers and some of the more energetic ones follow the practice of directing numerous letters of protest to editors but signing a different name to each.

Members of Congress are well aware of Communists starting their pressure campaigns by an avalanche of mail which follows the party line.

Radio

The party has departed from depending upon the printed word as its medium of propaganda and has taken to the air. Its members and sympathizers have not only infiltrated the airways but they are now persistently seeking radio channels.

Motion Pictures

The American Communists launched a furtive attack on Hollywood in 1935 by the issuance of a directive calling for a concentration in Hollywood. The orders called for action on two fronts. (1) An effort to infiltrate the labor unions; (2) infiltrate the so-called intellectual and creative fields.

In movie circles, Communists developed an effective defense a few years ago in meeting criticism. They would counter with the question, "After all, what is the matter with communism?" It was effective because many persons did not possess adequate knowledge of the subject to give an intelligent answer.

Some producers and studio heads realize the possibility that the entire industry faces serious embarrassment because it could become a springboard for Communist activities. Communist activity in Hollywood is effective and is furthered by Communists and sympathizers using the prestige of prominent persons to serve, often unwittingly, the Communist cause.

The party is content and highly pleased if it is possible to have inserted in a picture a line, a scene, a sequence, conveying the Communist lesson, and more particularly, if they can keep out anti-Communist lessons.

Infiltration

The Communist tactic of infiltrating labor unions stems from the earliest teachings of Marx, which have been reiterated by party spokesmen down through the years. They resort to all means to gain their point and often succeed in penetrating and literally taking over labor unions before the rank and file of members are aware of what has occurred. . . .

If more union members took a more active role and asserted themselves it would become increasingly difficult for Communists to gain control. Patriotic union members can easily spot sympathizers and party members in conventions and union meetings because invariably the latter strive to establish the party line instead of serving the best interests of the union and the country.

Foreign Language Groups

The party for the past 18 months has been giving special attention to foreign-language groups and has called for a sweeping self-critical examination of its work in this field. As long ago as 1945, in urging the importance of penetrating these groups, party leaders said, "We need only mention the Polish, Italian, Yugoslav, and Greek questions," and in characteristic party double talk observed that they occupied an important relationship "to the entire democratic camp and to the broader peoples movements." In other words, the Communists now seek strength from foreign groups who may have relatives in countries which Russia seeks to influence.

Government

The recent Canadian spy trials revealed the necessity of alertness in keeping Communists and sympathizers out of Government services. In fact, the high command of the Communist Party regards such assignments of sufficient importance to demand that party members not contact fellow members in the Government and if such Government employees are carried on party rolls at all they are assigned an alias. Last fall a high-ranking party leader instructed that all party membership cards of Government employees be destroyed and that party organizational meetings in Government circles are too obvious to mention.

There has developed, however, as a result of Communist propaganda, some fanciful feeling among Communists that no distinction should be drawn and that Communists have a right to Government jobs. I disagree in that. . . .

Mass and Front Organizations

The united-front program of the Communist Party was launched at the seventh world congress of the Communist International in 1935. The Communist Party in the United States immediately took up the program and a systematic plan was worked out of infiltrating existing organizations with Communists.

For the most part, front organizations assumed the character of either a mass or membership organization or a paper organization. Both solicited and used names of prominent persons. Literally hundreds of groups and organizations have either been infiltrated or organized primarily to accomplish the purposes of promoting the interests of the Soviet Union in the United States, the promotion of Soviet war and peace aims, the exploitation of Negroes in the United States, work among foreign-language groups, and to secure a favorable viewpoint toward the Communists in domestic, political, social, and economic issues.

The first requisite for front organizations is an idealistic sounding title. Hundreds of such organizations have come into being and have gone out of existence when their true purposes have become known or exposed while others with high-sounding names are continually springing up. . . .

The Test of a Front Organization

I feel that this committee could render a great service to the Nation through its power of exposure in quickly spotlighting existing front organizations and those which will be created in the future.

There are easy tests to establish the real character of such organizations:

1. Does the group espouse the cause of Americanism or the cause of Soviet Russia?

2. Does the organization feature as speakers at its meetings known Communists, sympathizers, or fellow travelers?

3. Does the organization shift when the party line shifts?

4. Does the organization sponsor causes, campaigns, literature, petitions, or other activities sponsored by the party or other front organizations?

5. Is the organization used as a sounding board by or is it endorsed by Communist-controlled labor unions?

6. Does its literature follow the Communist line or is it printed by the Communist press?

7. Does the organization receive consistent favorable mention in Communist publications?

8. Does the organization present itself to be nonpartisan yet engage in political activities and consistently advocate causes favored by the Communists?

9. Does the organization denounce American and British foreign policy while always lauding Soviet policy?

10. Does the organization utilize Communist "double talk" by referring to Soviet-dominated countries as democracies, complaining that the United States is imperialistic and constantly denouncing monopoly-capital?

11. Have outstanding leaders in public life openly renounced affiliation with the organization?

12. Does the organization, if espousing liberal progressive causes, attract well-known honest patriotic liberals or does it denounce well-known liberals?

13. Does the organization have a consistent record of supporting the American viewpoint over the years?

14. Does the organization consider matters not directly related to its avowed purposes and objectives?

National Defense

The Communist Party of the United States is a fifth column if there ever was one. It is far better organized than were the Nazis in occupied countries prior to their capitulation.

They are seeking to weaken America just as they did in their era of obstruction when they were alined with the Nazis. Their goal is the overthrow of our Government.

There is no doubt as to where a real Communist's loyalty rests. Their allegiance is to Russia, not the United States. . . .

What to Do

What can we do? And what should be our course of action? The best antidote to communism is vigorous, intelligent, old-fashioned Americanism with eternal vigilance. I do not favor any course of action which would give the Communists cause to portray and pity themselves as martyrs. I do favor unrelenting prosecution wherever they are found to be violating our country's laws.

As Americans, our most effective defense is a workable democracy that guarantees and preserves our cherished freedoms.

I would have no fears if more Americans possessed the zeal, the fervor, the persistence, and the industry to learn about this menace of Red fascism. I do fear for the liberal and progressive who has been hoodwinked and duped into joining hands with the Communists. I confess to a real apprehension so long as Communists are able to secure ministers of the gospel to promote their evil work and espouse a cause that is alien to the religion of Christ and Judaism. I do fear so long as school boards and parents tolerate conditions whereby Communists and fellow travelers, under the guise of academic freedom, can teach our youth a way of life that eventually will destroy the sanctity of the home, that undermines faith in God, that causes them to scorn respect for constituted authority and sabotage our revered Constitution.

I do fear so long as American labor groups are infiltrated, dominated or saturated with the virus of communism. I do fear the palliation and weasel-worded gestures against communism indulged in by some of our labor leaders who should know better but who have become pawns in the hands of sinister but astute manipulators for the Communist cause.

I fear for ignorance on the part of all our people who may take the poisonous pills of Communist propaganda.

I am deeply concerned whenever I think of the words of an old-time Communist. Disillusioned, disgusted and frightened he came to us with his story and concluded:

God help America or any other country if the Communist Party ever gets strong enough to control labor and politics.
God help us all!

The Communists have been, still are, and always will be a menace to freedom, to democratic ideals, to the worship of God and to America's way of life.

I feel that once public opinion is thoroughly aroused as it is today, the fight against communism is well on its way. Victory will be assured once Communists are identified and exposed, because the public will take the first step of quarantining them so they can do no harm. Communism, in reality, is not a political party. It is a way of life — an evil and malignant way of life. It reveals a condition akin to disease that spreads like an epidemic and like an epidemic a quarantine is necessary to keep it from infecting the Nation.

Suggestions for Additional Reading

Works which deal directly with the loyalty problem as defined in this volume are, almost without exception, highly argumentative. Among the book-length treatments of the subject, three should be especially mentioned here. Carey McWilliams, *Witch Hunt: The Revival of Heresy* (Boston, 1950), portions of which have been used in this book, is provocative throughout and is, of course, opposed to virtually every type of loyalty program. Alan Barth, in *The Loyalty of Free Men* (New York, 1951), subjects loyalty programs to severe and brilliantly written criticism, while Nathaniel Weyl in *The Battle against Disloyalty* (New York, 1951) gives a useful review of "fifth-column" activities in this country since revolutionary times and analyzes current loyalty programs with considerably more sympathy than does Barth or McWilliams. Among the many articles dealing with the problem within a smaller compass are George F. Kennan, "Where Do You Stand on Communism?" (*New York Times Magazine*, May 27, 1951); Laurence Sears, "Security and Liberty" (*American Scholar*, Vol. 20, No. 2, Spring, 1951, pp. 137–149); and Robert Bendiner, "Has Anti-Communism Wrecked Our Liberties?" (*Commentary*, Vol. 12, July, 1951, pp. 10–16). Rebecca West, *The Meaning of Treason* (New York, 1947), offers a highly thoughtful account of the case of Nazi-servant William Joyce (Lord Haw-Haw), whose behavior may profitably be compared with the alleged disloyalty of those who are today the chief object of loyalty programs.

For a more detailed investigation of the Communist Party and its activities in America, the reader may begin with the Report of Subcommittee No. 5 of the House Committee on Foreign Affairs, entitled *The Strategy and Tactics of World Communism* (House Document No. 619, 80th Congress, 2d Session; Washington, 1948), which contains a useful compilation of major Communist documents, and a Report of the House Committee on Un-American Activities entitled *The Communist Party of the United States as Agent of a Foreign Power* (House Document No. 209, 80th Congress, 1st Session; Washington, 1947). An official statement of the Communist attitude toward such reports can be found in Eugene Dennis, *Is Communism Un-American?* (New York, 1947). Chapter 23 of Martin Ebon, *World Communism Today* (New York, 1948), discusses the history and role of the party in this country. *The Communist Problem in America* (New York, 1951), a book of readings edited by Edward A. Palmer, also contains several articles of interest on this subject, as well as further materials on some of the issues discussed in this volume.

A number of more "intimate" books in recent decades have dealt with Communist and subversive activities with varying degrees of luridness. Elizabeth Dilling, *The Red Network* (Chicago, 1934); Robert L. Stripling, *The Red Plot against*

America (Drexel Hill, Pa., 1949); Martin Dies, *The Trojan Horse in America* (New York, 1940); Louis Budenz, *This Is My Story* (New York, 1947); and Benjamin Gitlow, *The Whole of Their Lives* (New York, 1948) are among the best known of these. The reliability of all of them, of course, is subject to varying interpretation, but the allegations, denials, and interpretations offered in such works as these are themselves an important part of the present-day loyalty problem.

There are many works dealing in some detail with particular dramatic incidents connected with the problem in recent years. Among those of interest here are Bert Andrews, *Washington Witch Hunt* (New York, 1948), dealing with some revelations of the House Committee on Un-American Activities; Alistair Cooke, *A Generation on Trial* (New York, 1950), dealing with the case of Alger Hiss; Ralph De Toledano and Victor Lasky, *Seeds of Treason* (New York, 1950), also concerning the Hiss Case; Gordon Kahn, *Hollywood on Trial*, about the writers indicted for contempt of Congress; and Owen Lattimore, *Ordeal by Slander* (Boston, 1950), which offers Lattimore's reply to the charges made by Senator McCarthy.

Further discussion of the specific issues treated in the present volume is to be found primarily in periodicals. There is a wealth of material dealing with judicial and constitutional aspects of the case of the Communist "politburo" in many of the leading law reviews. A classic survey of the issues involved, as presented in outstanding previous cases, is to be found in Zechariah Chafee, *Free Speech in the United States* (Cambridge, Mass., 1946).

For a fuller understanding of the federal government's loyalty program, the reader should begin with a study of the order creating this program, Executive Order No. 9835 (*Federal Register*, Vol. 12, p. 1935; Washington, 1947). There is an exhaustive analysis of the program, hostile to it, by Thomas I. Emerson and David M. Helfeld under the title, "Loyalty among Government Employees" (*Yale Law Journal*, Vol. 58, December, 1948, pp. 1–143), a reply to this article by J. Edgar Hoover under the title, "A Comment on the Article, 'Loyalty among Government Employees'" (*Yale Law Journal*, Vol. 58, February, 1949, pp. 401–411), and a further reply and rejoinder by each party (*Yale Law Journal*, Vol. 58, February, 1949, pp. 412–425). William J. Donovan and Mary Gardiner Jones, in "Program for a Democratic Counter-Attack to Communist Penetration of Government Service" (*Yale Law Journal*, Vol. 58, July, 1949, pp. 1211–1241), survey the program and offer some interesting suggestions for one they believe is more likely to meet the demands of security, liberty, and efficient government service. Walter Gellhorn, in *Security, Loyalty and Science* (Ithaca, N. Y., 1950), deals with security and loyalty problems as related to the effort to safeguard information of a secret or confidential nature.

Further study of the McCarran Act should begin with the text of the entire Act (Public Law 831, 81st Congress; Chapter 1024, 2d Session). The reader should also consult reports of Congressional committee hearings on this bill and its numerous predecessors. The article by Arthur E. Sutherland, Jr., "Freedom and Internal Security" (*Harvard Law Review*, Vol. 64, January, 1951, pp. 383–416), parts of which have been included in this volume, is worth reading in its entirety. H. B. Kirshen, "The Internal Security Act of 1950" (*American Association of University Professors Bulletin*,

Vol. 37, Summer, 1951, pp. 260–275), is highly critical of the Act, and Zechariah Chafee, "Freedom and Fear" (*American Association of University Professors Bulletin,* Vol. 35, Autumn, 1949, pp. 398–433), criticizes provisions of the Mundt-Johnson Bill which were later incorporated in the McCarran Act.

The reader will find further development of Sidney Hook's views concerning Communists' participation in academic pursuits in "The Danger of Authoritarian Attitudes in Teaching Today" (*School and Society,* Vol. 73, January 20, 1951, pp. 33–39); "What Shall We Do about Communist Teachers?" (*Saturday Evening Post,* Vol. 222, September 10, 1949, pp. 33 ff.); and "Academic Confusions" (*Journal of Higher Education,* Vol. 20, November, 1949, pp. 422–425). Alexander Meiklejohn's views are further developed, in a somewhat wider context, in *Freedom and the College* (New York, 1923), *What Does America Mean?* (New York, 1935), and *Free Speech and Its Relation to Self-Government* (New York, 1948). Carl J. Friedrich, "Teachers' Oaths" (*Harper's,* Vol. 172, January, 1936, pp. 171–177), is especially interesting here, inasmuch as it was written during a somewhat earlier period of concern over subversion in the schools. The *American Scholar Forum* (Vol. 18, Summer, 1948) contains a stimulating set of controversial articles relating particularly to the so-called Washington University case. The *American Association of University Professors Bulletin* contains many discussions of the academic aspect of the loyalty problem, among them Alan Barth, "The Loyalty of Free Men" (Vol. 37, Spring, 1951, pp. 5–16), which looks at the academic problem from the viewpoint expressed in his book of the same title; Lyle Owen, "Communism and Our Colleges" (Vol. 36, Autumn, 1950, pp.

437–446); and DR Scott, "The Rationale of Academic Freedom" (Vol. 36, Winter, 1950, pp. 629–645). The *Journal of Higher Education, School and Society,* and other specialized periodicals likewise contain many articles dealing with this particular aspect of the loyalty problem.

Publications which tend to support a particular viewpoint (such as *Catholic World, Commonweal, The Nation, The New Republic,* and others) are worth consulting for the presentation of their views on both the various specific aspects and upon the general problem.

A widely discussed problem not directly treated in this volume, but intimately related to those which are treated, concerns the activities of the House Committee on Un-American Activities. This problem is discussed in Walter Gellhorn's "Report on a Report of the House Committee on Un-American Activities" (*Harvard Law Review,* Vol. 60, October, 1947, pp. 1193–1234), and A. J. Liebling's *Mink and Red Herring* (New York, 1949). The reports and records of the Committee itself should, of course, be consulted. Concerning proposals to outlaw the Communist Party, there is an excellent collection of articles in Julia E. Johnsen, *Should the Communist Party Be Outlawed?* (*The Reference Shelf,* Vol. 20, No. 7; New York, 1949). Activities of a more local nature than those discussed in this book are surveyed in William B. Prendergast, "State Legislatures and Communism: The Current Scene" (*American Political Science Review,* Vol. 44, September, 1950, pp. 556–574).

As has repeatedly been emphasized, the loyalty problem cannot be intelligently discussed solely in terms of the technicalities involved in the particular measures treated above. Merle Curti, *The Roots of American Loyalty* (New York, 1946), and Percy Holmes Boynton,

Changing Ideals of American Patriotism (Chicago, 1936), will afford opportunity for the reader to examine again, in the light of historical experience, the basic question: What is loyalty to America? Of particular interest here, too, are the articles by Charles C. Marshall, "An Open Letter to the Honorable Alfred E. Smith" (*Atlantic Monthly*, Vol. 139, April, 1927, pp. 540–549), and Alfred E. Smith, "Catholic and Patriot: Governor Smith Replies" (*Atlantic Monthly*, Vol. 139, May, 1927, pp. 721–728), concerning the charges made by Marshall that Governor Smith's religious loyalty precluded his serving loyally as the nation's president. Josiah Royce, *The Philosophy of Loyalty* (New York, 1908), and Herbert Aaron Bloch, *The Concept of Our Changing Loyalties* (New York, 1934), offer analyses in terms of general philosophy and social psychology, respectively, which are directly pertinent to the basic question in this problem. The Brookings Institution report, *Suggested Standards for Determining Un-Americanism* (Washington, 1945), prepared at the request of the House Committee, is an interesting attempt to give a specific answer to that question.